HISTORY OF NURSE-MIDWIFERY
IN THE UNITED STATES

BY

SISTER M. THEOPHANE SHOEMAKER

———

𝔄 𝔇issertation

SUBMITTED TO THE FACULTY OF THE SCHOOL OF NURSING EDUCATION
OF THE CATHOLIC UNIVERSITY OF AMERICA, IN PARTIAL
FULFILLMENT OF THE REQUIREMENTS FOR THE
DEGREE OF MASTER OF SCIENCE

———

THE CATHOLIC UNIVERSITY OF AMERICA PRESS
WASHINGTON, D. C.

To

OUR LADY, CAUSE OF OUR JOY

and

To All the Medical Mission Sisters Who Were
Living in Washington During the Time
This Thesis Was Being Written

TABLE OF CONTENTS

LIST OF TABLES

INTRODUCTION

The purpose of this study is to investigate the general circumstances which led to the introduction of nurse-midwifery into the United States, to trace the development of nurse-midwifery in the United States from its inception to the present time, and to discover those factors which have exercised the greatest influence in its development.

This topic was chosen by the writer for three reasons: first, because of her interest as a nurse-midwife in this particular branch of nursing; second, because no one has written a complete history of nurse-midwifery in the United States up to this time; and lastly, because there is a need for such an account that can be given to students as a reference.

In order to clarify the meaning of *nurse-midwifery* it is necessary to define three terms: *obstetrics, midwifery,* and finally *nurse-midwifery.*

Doctor Dorland's *Medical Dictionary* defines *obstetrics* as "The art of managing childbirth cases; that branch of surgery which deals with the management of pregnancy and labor.[1] *Webster's Dictionary* says it is the "science of midwifery; art of assisting women in parturition; the management of pregnancy and labor."[2] The same medical dictionary does not define *midwifery* but refers the reader to *obstetrics* implying that the two words are synonymous, while Webster's Dictionary gives as a definition the "art, practice, act, or fact of assisting at childbirth,"[3] which is not different from that of *obstetrics* in the same book.

Although officially midwifery and obstetrics are synonymous, here has developed in the minds of Americans a distinction between their meanings as is brought out by the literature.[4] However,

---

[1] W. A. Dorland, *The American Illustrated Medical Dictionary,* (19th ed.; Philadelphia: W. B. Saunders Co., 1942), p. 992.

[2] *Webster's New International Dictionary of the English Language,* (Springfield: G. & C. Merriam Co., 1911), p. 1485.

[3] *Ibid.,* p. 1369.

[4] Carrie M. Hall, "Training the Obstetrical Nurse," *American Journal of Nursing,* XXVII (1927), p. 374. Joseph B. DeLee, M.D., "Obstetrics Versus Midwifery," *Journal of the American Medical Association,* CIII (1934), p. 307.

because of the diversion of opinions regarding the application of these two terms in modern usage, we shall, for purposes of this study, use them synonymously.

Nurse-Midwifery is not defined in either dictionaries or writings on this subject, but the many descriptions of what the nurse-midwife is and what she does suggest the following interpretation of this term: Nurse-Midwifery is the art and science of obstetrics or midwifery as practiced by a graduate, registered, professional nurse who has taken a course in midwifery at a school for nurse-midwives and has met all the requirements for graduation and holds a diploma or certificate from her school. This is the meaning the term will connote when used in this study.

Midwifery or obstetrics in the United States is done by three groups: namely, physicians, nurse-midwives, and untrained or partially trained women who attend confinements in the neighborhood of their homes. The latter we shall refer to as native or indigenous midwives.

The factual data for this study was gathered from the literature and personal investigation by interviews and correspondence. More specifically, these sources are the following:

1. A review of the professional literature from 1900 to 1946, and of the articles written in books and periodicals by nurse-midwives about the activities of nurse-midwives. There were comparatively few references that afforded primary source material as will be seen by a review of the bibliography.

2. Interviews with the following nurses: Miss Hazel Corbin, Director of the Maternity Center Association in New York City; Miss Ruth Doran, Public Health Nursing Consultant, United States Children's Bureau, Washington, D. C., Miss Lalla Mary Goggans, Regional Nursing Consultant, United States Children's Bureau, Dallas, Texas; Miss Hattie Hemschemeyer, Assistant Director of the Maternity Center Association in New York City, and Director of the School of Nurse-Midwifery conducted by the same Association.

3. Correspondence with the Directors of Public Health Nursing in the forty-eight states and the District of Columbia. A letter

was written asking for information regarding: the date nurse-mid-wives were first employed; how many were employed at the present time; the titles of positions they were filling; if provision existed in the state for licensure of the nurse-midwife; what programs had been developed in which the nurse-midwives took a part, and for annual reports which gave information regarding these activities.

4. Correspondence with the directors of the existing schools for nurse-midwifery in the United States.

5. A review of nurse-midwifery school announcements and other publications, and unpublished materials about the nurse-midwifery schools in the United States.

6. An analysis of information supplied by specified schools covering educational status, agency or individual granting scholarships for nurse-midwifery study, and positions held since graduation.

An attempt has been made to report the findings of this study in the order that will enable the reader to follow with the clearest possible understanding and appreciation of the steps by which nurse-midwifery has developed in the United States. The first chapter covers the period during which the need for nurse-midwifery was discussed and the important activities that led up to the early attempts to provide a school in which to prepare nurse-midwives. The second chapter records the opening of the first nurse-midwifery program in the United States and its development; and the general program of public education on maternity, which paved the way for the first American school of nurse-midwifery.

Chapter three is the history of the first official school for nurse-midwifery. Chapter four deals with all other nurse-midwifery schools that have been opened in the United States. In Chapter five the activities of nurse-midwives in the various states have been organized, according to information revealed by the correspondence, interviews, bulletins, and unpublished material; and finally, chapter six recounts the development of nurse-midwifery organizations in the United States.

The writer hopes that this study will serve to encourage many well-qualified nurses to devote their lives to the promotion of health and happiness among mothers and babies in the whole world.

CHAPTER I

EARLY PERIOD

In the first decade of the twentieth century some areas of the United States were sufficiently stabilized and organized to permit systematic collection of statistical data regarding the salient features of maternal care. The collections were at best sketchy and not complete enough to give an accurate picture of the whole situation. Such information as was obtained, however, did indicate that obstetric conditions were far worse in the United States than they were in some of the European countries where a well-organized obstetric service was conducted by well-trained and licensed midwives.[1] In our larger cities a high percentage of the deliveries were conducted by indigenous midwives who had no training and no legal status. In New York City over 40 percent of the confinements were cared for by 3,121 untrained attendants.[2]

The conditions in other sections of the country which were less favored with facilities for modern health care were evidently worse. Moreover, studies made during the first few years of this century brought to the attention of the medical profession the exceedingly poor preparation that a large proportion of medical students received on obstetrics.[3] No legal standard had been set which would influence either physicians or native midwives in their care of maternity patients.

In an effort to establish a control over the activities of the native midwives, it had been suggested that they be given legal recognition by state licensure and be given some preparation for their work through the establishment of midwifery schools for them. This proposal met with vigorous opposition by some of the outstanding physicians in the field of obstetrics. The whole question of licensing and controlling the practice of the midwife became known as the

[1] Mary Beard, "Midwifery in England," *Public Health Nursing*, XVIII (1926), pp. 634-640.

[2] Josephine Baker, M.D., "The Function of the Midwife," *The Women's Medical Journal*, XXIII (1913), p. 196.

[3] J. Whitridge Williams, M.D., "Medical Education and the Midwife problem,"*Journal of the American Medical Association*, LVIII (1912, pp. 1-7.

midwife problem as the literature of the second decade and even on to the present time bear witness.

One of the conclusions drawn from an analysis of data obtained by J. Whitridge Williams, M.D. of Johns Hopkins University from forty-three professors of obstetrics in medical schools throughout the nation indicates the general feeling that prevailed among many physicians. "Reform is urgently needed, and can be accomplished more speedily by radical improvement in medical education than by attempting the almost impossible task of improving midwives."[4] C. E. Ziegler, M.D., professor of obstetrics at the University of Pittsburgh and Medical Director of the Elizabeth Steel Magee Hospital, said in regard to the midwife problem:

> . . . . My own feeling is that the great danger lies in the possibility of attempting to educate the midwife and in licensing her to practice midwifery, giving her thereby a legal status which later cannot perhaps be altered.
>
> .   .   .   .
>
> I am opposed to education and licensing midwives . . . . for several reasons; first, because I believe it unnecessary . . . . and second, because I do not believe it possible to train women of the type of even the best of midwives to practise obstetrics satisfactorily.[5]

Arthur Brewster Emmons, M.D., and James L. Huntington, M.D., of Boston prepared a paper which was read in the section of Midwifery of the American Association for the Study and Prevention of Infant Mortality held in Chicago in 1911, in which they denounced the midwife and refused to see in her any element of helpfulness.[6]

Many physicians concurred in this opinion. However, there were others who believed that if the midwife was licensed, trained, and properly supervised, she could fulfill an important function as an obstetric attendant and at the same time, by raising the standard of

---

[4] *Ibid.,* p. 6.

[5] Charles E. Ziegler, M.D., "The Elimination of the Midwife," *The Journal of the American Medical Association,* LX (1913), p. 32.

[6] Arthur B. Emmons, M.D., and James L. Huntington, M.D., "The Midwife," *The American Journal of Obstetrics and Diseases of Women and Children,* LXV (1912), p. 393.

care, help to reduce the maternal and infant mortality. One of the principal defendants of the midwives was a woman physician. Recognizing that these women had filled a need which it would have been impossible for physicians to fill in caring for the hundreds of thousands of confinements in the United States, and that this need would continue, Josephine S. Baker, M.D., of the Women's Medical College in Philadelphia said:

> . . . . so long as a considerable proportion of our population demands midwives, we will have them. If unlicensed and unsupervised, they will continue to practice and fail to report their births . . . . Properly educated and controlled, they have a distinct function of combining the features of a well trained attendant at normal child-birth, a teacher of proper baby care and a housewife.[7]

At a meeting of the American Association for the Study and Prevention of Infant Mortality, held in Chicago on November 18, 1911, Ira S. Wile, M.D., declared: "it is manifestly unfair to criticise the lack of an educational standard which has never been established . . . . Let there be an evolution of this class of public servants and not a hasty attempt to check their possible development."[8]

All of the physicians evidently acknowledged the unsatisfactory preparation medical schools were offering their students and the lack of possibility for the medical profession to shoulder the whole task of obstetric care. C. E. Ziegler, M.D., says that "midwifery is the most poorly done of all medical work."[9]

It was apparent that something had to be done to provide acceptable care to mothers and babies and care that would reduce the high mortality rates prevailing. Gradually some of the states were passing laws to provide for legal recognition of the native midwives with certain specified requirements to control their practice. Efforts were being made to raise the educational standards of the medical schools. It was in the course of this struggle that the question of the nurse-midwife was introduced. The nurse-midwife was

---

[7] Baker, *op. cit.*, p. 196.

[8] Ira S. Wile, M.D., "Schools for Midwives," *Medical Record,* LXXXI (1912), p. 517.

[9] Ziegler, *op. cit.,* p. 32.

already an established institution in European countries; so far there were none in the United States.

Clara D. Noyes, Superintendent of Training Schools, Bellevue and Allied Hospitals, New York, before the International Congress of Hygiene and Demography held in Washington in September, 1912 said:

> .... It is not improbable to expect that advanced obstetrical training will eventually be given to nurses in this country to fit them to carry their share in this problem of mothers and babies.
>
> If the midwife can gradually be replaced by the nurse who has, upon her general training super-imposed a course in practical midwifery, which has been clearly defined by obstetricians, it would seem a logical economic solution to the problem . . . . we should be able to provide better teaching, better nursing and eventually better medical assistance to the less highly favored classes.[10]

Following this address, many physicians when speaking about the obstetric problem, and its solution, mentioned the nurse along with the physician but the first whole-hearted acceptance of the idea of nurse-midwifery as a part of the obstetric scheme that the writer was able to find, was that of Fred J. Taussig, M.D., of St. Louis. At the Second Annual Meeting of the National Organization of Public Health Nurses held on April 25, 1914, he spoke as follows:

> As an important step in the solution of this problem, I would suggest for your consideration that the establishment of schools of midwifery, admission to which would be limited to graduate nurses. . . .
>
> My idea of the curriculum of such a school would include the following: Attendance for six months to a year, entire charge of at least thirty cases of normal confinement, a majority of which should be out-clinic cases, a systematic course of lectures and demonstrations, through hospital training in diagnosis, special work in the treatment of emergencies. . . .
>
> · · · · · · · · ·
>
> .... Under the system of the nurse-midwife, she would

---

[10] Clara D. Noyes, R.N., "The Training of Midwives in Relation to the Prevention of Infant Mortality," *The American Journal of Obstetrics and Diseases of Women and Children,* LXVI (1912), p. 1051.

also undertake some of the work of the physician. In the vast majority of cases the latter could be spared the necessity of attending confinements.[11]

Although he appreciated the part a nurse, properly prepared, could take in caring for maternity patients, he saw that it would take time. He added:

> In conclusion, if I have been over enthusiastic on the subject of schools of nurse-midwifery, it is with a realization that changes of this sort are not made in a day, but are the result of gradual evolution. It will take many schools many years to supplant all the midwives, but eventually it will come to pass. The nurse-midwife will, I believe, prove to be the most sympathetic, the most economical, and the most efficient agent in the case of normal confinements.[12]

Although the idea of the nurse-midwife had been introduced, no actual steps were taken to open the field of nurse-midwifery for several years. The writer was unable to find any allusion to the subject between the years 1914 and 1923 in professional literature. Nevertheless, other steps were taken to study the obstetric needs of the country and to fill them in what seemed to be the best possible way which prepared the way for the introduction of the nurse-midwife.

In 1912 the Federal Government established the United States Children's Bureau in the Department of Labor by an Act approved on April 9 of that year, and among the functions of this Bureau was to "investigate and report . . . . upon all matters pertaining to the welfare of children and child life among all classes of people, and shall especially investigate the questions of infant mortality, the birth rate . . . ."[13] This provision led to further study of the actual conditions of maternal and infant care throughout the country and the death rates among mothers and babies. The reports from

[11] Fred J. Taussig, M.D., *The Nurse-Midwife* (Paper read at the Second Annual Meeting of the National Organization for Public Health Nurses, April 25, 1914), p. 2.

[12] *Ibid.*, p. 4.

[13] Katherine F. Lenroot, *The Children's Bureau* (Washington, D. C.: U. S. Department of Labor), p. 16.

these studies showed a need of financial assistance from the Federal Government. In an effort to supply this need, a bill was introduced into Congress which called for money to pay for better care to mothers and babies and specified that public health nurses should be employed for the instruction of the untrained midwives. This bill was passed as the Sheppard-Towner Act in November 1921. These funds were to be administered by the United States Children's Bureau through the State Department of Health.[14]

Besides these federal laws, more and more of the states were passing laws to regulate educational standards, examinations, practice, registration, licensing, and penalties for violation of the native midwives.[15] These laws worked simultaneously to improve the obstetric care for a large number of mothers and their babies. As a result of these requirements for practice, several schools were established to enable the native midwives to meet them. Of these schools two were outstanding and remained in existance over a fairly long period.[16] One of these was the Bellevue School of Midwifery in New York City. It was supported by city taxes and remained open from 1911 until 1935 when it was closed because the need for native midwives was no longer felt.[17] The other school that is mentioned most frequently in the literature is that connected with the Preston Retreat Hospital in Philadelphia, which was opened in 1923. The hospital had been built in 1836 for indigent married women of that city and is an all-charity institution where no medical students are allowed to care for patients. The school has remained open to the present time although few students have taken the course since 1930.[18]

Another important institution that was destined to play a leading

[14] Obstetric Education—A Report of the Subcommittee on Obstetric Teaching and Education of the White House Conference, (New York: The Century Co., 1932), p. 237.

[15] Anna E. Rude, M.D., "The Midwife Problem in the United States," (Paper read before the Section on Obstetrics and Gynecology and Abdominal Surgery in San Francisco, June 1923), p. 10.

[16] Obstetric Education, *op. cit.*, pp. 192-195.

[17] George W. Kosmak, M.D., "The Midwife," *Briefs*, VIII, No. 5 (1945).

[18] Letter from Stella Mummert, Superintendent of Preston Retreat, June 24, 1946.

part in preparing the way for the nurse-midwife was the Maternity Center Association in New York City. It came into existence as a result of a study inaugurated by the Health Commissioner of New York City in 1915. The purpose of the study to "analyze the existing conditions surrounding women in childbirth in Manhattan . . . . revealed that many deaths were caused by lack of prenatal care of any kind and of poor care at the time of delivery."[19] As a result a plan was made by which the city should be zoned and in each zone a center for maternity care should be established.

The first center opened in 1917 and was sponsored by the Women's City Club. Additional centers were opened later by the New York Milk Committee.[20] As these centers developed, there developed also a need for central and vigorous organization and this need resulted in the establishment of the Maternity Center Association in April, 1918, with Frances Perkins its first Director. She filled this office until 1920 when Anne Stephens replaced her. Hazel Corbin became the Director in 1923 and has held the same position since that time.[21]

By 1920 the Association had thirty maternity centers in New York. In 1921, by an experiment worked out with the Henry Street Visiting Nurse Association, Maternity Center showed that specialized supervision of maternity work carried on in a generalized public health nursing program was of special value. During this same year the officers of the Association believed that all nursing agencies and hospitals caring for families in Manhattan were given sufficient emphasis to prenatal care to justify abandoning its scattered effort in the many centers and concentrating its facilities to give a complete maternity service in one small district. The co-operation of all physicians and agencies in the district were solicited and during the period of the demonstration, the nurses on the staff of the Maternity Center Association proved their missionary spirit by a service of a self-sacrifice attending clinics, giving care and instruction in the home or hospital, day or night, as the need arose.

[19] *Maternity Center Association 1918-1943,* (New York: Maternity Center Association, 1943), pp. 20-21.

[20] *Ibid.,* p. 21.

[21] Information obtained from Hazel Corbin, (personal interview).

Everything was done to assure every mother in the district the best care that could possibly be provided. At the same time an effort was made to supply information to expectant parents throughout the United States about the need for maternity care. This was the first attempt to reach the public at large, outside of Manhattan Island.[22]

A rigid and continuous staff education program for the nurses on the staff of the Association was conducted and many nurses from public health agencies throughout the country came to spend some time with the Association for experience under its supervision and to learn its methods. Exhibits were constructed for teaching purposes and were provided, upon request, to individuals or agencies for the same purpose.[23]

The experience of the nurses in this program of maternity care and education from 1921 to 1923, revealed some problems which served to convince the Board of Directors of the Maternity Center Association that it would be useful to train nurses to do normal obstetrics.[24] In 1923, with this in mind, they worked out a plan with the Bellevue School of Midwifery, which had been operating since 1911 for the training of native midwives, by which nurses would be prepared to do midwifery. This project was relinquished because the New York City Commissioner of Welfare refused to cooperate.[25]

Undaunted by this disappointment during the same year, the Association called a meeting of obstetricians and public health nursing executives to study the value of the nurse-midwife and to determine whether or not this group believed that a training center should be established for such education. The Maternity Center Association records that ". . . . it was a bitter meeting, for a number of the leaders of obstetrics and nursing believed that there was no place for the nurse-midwife, and declared the time had come when we must eliminate midwifery entirely from our social scheme."[26] Furthermore "fear of medical-nursing relationships made the nurs-

[22] *Maternity Center Association 1918-1943, op. cit.,* pp. 55, 57.

[23] *Ibid.,* p. 56.

[24] Information obtained from Hazel Corbin, (personal interview).

[25] *Maternity Center Association 1918-1943, op. cit.,* p. 25.

[26] *Ibid.,* p. 25.

ing representatives hesitant to lend the support of the public health nursing movement, then in its infancy."[27] Such opposition convinced the Maternity Center Association that the time was not yet right for the opening of a school of nurse-midwifery. Without giving up hope it put the idea aside temporarily and launched on other new and challenging projects to promote maternity which presented greater immediate possibility.[28]

[27] Hattie Hemschemeyer, "Midwifery in the United States," *The American Journal of Nursing*, XXXIX (1939), p. 1186.

[28] *Maternity Center Association 1918-1943, op. cit.,* pp. 59-66.

CHAPTER II

Although the Maternity Center Association in New York was the first organized group to see nurse-midwifery as an asset in the obstetric program and to introduce a definite plan for such training, the acclaim for initiating a nurse-midwifery program in the United States must go to Mrs. Mary Breckinridge of Kentucky. It was a new program in a frontier territory and showed results that were well worth while.

Mrs. Breckinridge was a native of Kentucky[1] and had always been interested in the welfare of mothers and babies in her home state. She was graduated from St. Luke's Hospital School of Nursing in New York and was married following graduation. The loss of two children fortified her resolve to use her nursing for the promotion of health and happiness among mothers in remote areas.[2] For this purpose she went to Boston and took a period of training in public health nursing under Anne Strong and Mary Beard. Following this she went to Europe and spent the years from 1919 to 1922 in organizing the Visiting Nurse Service of the American Committee for Devastated France and as Director of Child Hygiene and Public Health Nursing for that Committee.[3]

Meanwhile she had not forgotten America's neglected mothers and babies. When she returned to this country in 1922 she spent one year at Teacher's College, Columbia University in New York studying public health nursing.[4] When the year was over she returned to Kentucky to begin her work.

Realizing that in order to meet the needs of the mothers she must first know what the needs were, Mrs. Breckinridge began by mak-

---

[1] Mary Breckinridge, "Midwifery in the Kentucky Mountains, An Investigation in 1923," *The Quarterly Bulletin of the Frontier Nursing Service,* XVII, No. 4 (1942), p. 30.

[2] *Ibid.*

[3] "Mary Breckenridge, R.N., Nurse-Midwife," *The American Journal of Nursing* XXX (1930), p. 311.

[4] *Ibid.*

ing a thorough investigation of the status of obstetric care in three counties located in the heart of the Kentucky Mountains. This study was planned in cooperation with Doctor Arthur McCormack, State Health Officer of Kentucky, and carried out with his full approval. The area studied covered approximately one thousand square miles with a population of 29,572 according to the 1920 census.[5] The three largest towns in the area had populations of 313,467, and 243 respectively. No railroads or automobile roads entered the territory. The customary mode of travel was on horseback following "such roads or trails as exist, through the creek beds, up the branches, over the gaps and ridges of the mountains."[6]

From July to late September, 1923, Mrs. Breckinridge spent traveling to every corner of the three counties, questioning native midwives, talking with mothers and their families. Part of the time she was accompanied by Miss Ella Woodyard of the Institute of Educational Research of Teachers College who took individual mental tests on the mountain children between the ages of six and ten. Mrs. Breckinridge wanted to know if isolation or a lack of native intelligence were responsible for the poor health conditions among these people.[7]

The scope of this study does not permit the recounting of all the details of the investigation but some of the findings are of particular importance. During the year 1922 ". . . . 968 births had been reported for this territory, and that reported deliveries had been made by nine doctors, not all of whom were state licensed, and 128 midwives. Twenty other midwives had not reported their cases. Since the average age of fifty-three of the midwives, who were personally interviewed, was 60.3, it was obvious that this could not be considered a teaching group."[8] Four conclusions were drawn from the

[5] Mary Breckinridge, "Midwifery in the Kentucky Mountains, An Investigation in 1923," *The Quarterly Bulletin of the Frontier Nursing Service,* XVII, No. 4 (1942), p. 32.

[6] *Ibid.,* p. 33.

[7] *Ibid.,* p. 30

[8] "Mary Breckinridge, R.N., Nurse-Midwife," *The American Journal of Nursing* XXX (1930), pp. 311-312.

study which guided Mrs. Breckinridge in formulating a plan by which to proceed:

> 1. Persons attempting to serve the group must be so situated that they would be available within reasonable time, hence a decentralized service was needed.
> 2. The existing supply of doctors . . . . was entirely inadequate.
> 3. The number of midwives would be reduced three-fourths if young and well mounted.
> 4. Because of the way babies have of coming in clumps, two attendants would be necessary for each unit of space to be covered, and not all of their time would be needed for midwifery.[9]

These conclusions led Mrs. Breckinridge to decide to study midwifery. Since there was no school for nurse-midwifery in America she was obliged to go to England. After having completed the midwifery course at the York Road Lying-In Hospital in London, she took a teaching course for midwives through the Midwives' Institute, British Hospital, Woolwich, London. She was certified by the Central Midwives Board and was the first American Nurse-Midwife. Following this preparation for midwifery in London, she went to Scotland and spent some time observing the medical and nursing service which had been established in the highlands and islands by Sir Leslie McKenzie.[10]

All of this was preliminary to giving skilled care to the mothers and babies in the Kentucky mountains; they were still receiving the type of obstetric care they had always received. But they were not to wait for long.

On returning to the United States and to Kentucky Mrs. Breckinridge immediately began to interest her friends and other prominent Kentuckians in the health program she contemplated for the neglected mountain women and children.

On May 28, 1925, the results of her hard labors took on concrete form when a group of individuals met in Frankfort and established

[9] *Ibid.*, p. 312.
[10] *Ibid.*, p. 312.

the Kentucky Committee for Mothers and Babies. The purpose of the Committee was formulated as follows:

> To safeguard the lives and health of mothers and young children by providing trained nurse-midwives for rural areas where there are no resident physicians—these nurse-midwives to work under supervision; in compliance with the Regulations for midwives of the State Board of Health, and the law governing the Registration of Nurses in Kentucky; and in cooperation with the nearest medical service.[11]

The general working plan was laid down: The work would be carried out from special nursing centers, in each of which two nurse-midwives would reside. The centers would be spaced to give the nurses in each center a population they could handle well on horseback.[12] It was decided that special attention would be given to maternity and infant care, while carrying on a generalized public health nursing program.

During 1925 the members of the Kentucky Committee numbered sixty-three, all but six were residents of Kentucky; the others were from New York, Chicago, Pennsylvania, Virginia, West Virginia, and Washington, D. C. All were outstanding citizens and six were physicians.[13]

The summer of 1925 was devoted to a concentrated and detailed survey of Leslie County where the Committee had decided the work should begin. This survey was conducted under the direction of Miss Bertram Ireland, a Scotch woman, who was employed by the Committee on Maternal Health in New York, and was lent to the Kentucky Committee for this purpose.[14] An account of the study is published in the second issue of the Bulletin, *The Kentucky Committee for Mothers and Babies*, October, 1925.

As Mrs. Breckinridge opened her first nursing center on Sep-

[11] "Midwifery in Kentucky," *The American Journal of Nursing*, XXV (1925), p. 1004.

[12] *Ibid.*

[13] "Members," *The Kentucky Committee for Mothers and Babies*, I, No. 2 (1925), p. 2.

[14] "The Survey," *The Kentucky Committee for Mothers and Babies*, I, No. 2 (1925), p. 4.

tember 1, 1925 at Hyden, Leslie County, Kentucky,[15] she knew that many of the questions that were in her mind would soon begin to be answered. She did not know whether her nurse-midwives would be able to reduce the maternal and infant mortality to a rate comparable to that of England, and other European countries. Neither was she sure the nurse-midwives would be willing to work year after year in such an isolated and remote area; or if the people so unused to professional care would accept it. The cost of the service would have to be financed and just how this would and could be done was an open question. From the outset it was in the plan to answer these questions by scientifically accurate records.[16]

In order to assure that the program was understood by the local people for whom the service was established, a meeting was called on August 22, 1925 and to this group the plan of the Kentucky Committee was thoroughly explained. Those present were much impressed and formed themselves into a Branch Committee, setting up resolutions by which they promised to support the work, to hold regular meetings for this purpose, and specified that a fee of $5.00 would be required of all who could afford to pay for the service.[17]

The first nursing center was housed in a rented building in Hyden, Kentucky and the first employed nurse-midwives were American nurses who had gone to England at Mrs. Breckenridge's persuasion to study midwifery. By the end of the first month of activity, twenty patients were registered for care at confinement and four of the twenty had delivered.[18]

This first center was developing rapidly in its clientele when the second center opened at Wendover. This center, located about 14 miles from Hyden was to be the home of Mrs. Breckinridge and the general headquarters of the service and for guests. By the

[15] "The First Centers of Nurse-Midwifery," *The Kentucky Committee for Mothers and Babies*, I, No. 2 (1925), p. 12.

[16] "Our Objectives," *The Kentucky Committee for Mothers and Babies*, I, No. 2 (1925), pp. 13-14.

[17] "Resolutions," *The Kentucky Committee for Mothers and Babies*, I, No. 2 (1925), pp. 15-17.

[18] "The First Centers of Nurse-Midwifery," *The Kentucky Committee for Mothers and Babies*, I, No. 2 (1925), p. 12.

fall of 1926 the third center was established by Miss Mary B. Willeford and Miss Gladys Peacock who had recently returned from their midwifery studies in England.[19]

Each succeeding center was backed by a well-organized local committee of citizens. The plan of organization was the same in each area.

All the while Mrs. Breckinridge bore the responsibility of the general direction of the work. It was she who got enough money together to pay the bills, who sought for people of wealth who would donate the cost of nursing centers and, when possible, to endow them. The publication of the Quarterly Bulletin was an undertaking suggested to her by the Executive Group. Besides these offices she acted as general supervisor to the nurse-midwives, wrote articles for publication, and gave talks at meetings wherever and whenever it was possible in order to make the work known and to interest the people of America in financing it. When she was at home, she was hostess to numerous guests.

As the work expanded, not only did more American nurses go to England for the course in midwifery, but a large number of midwives from England and Scotland came to join the nursing staff. Most of the nurses who went from the United States to study in England were granted scholarships by the Committee. Each nurse to come was introduced to readers of the Bulletin of the service.

During the first two years the nurse-midwives worked in Kentucky, whenever necessity for hospitalization arose, patients were sent to Hazard, twenty-four miles from Hyden, or to Lexington much farther away. In 1927, however, plans were made by the Executive Committee to build a small hospital at Hyden, in connection with the first nursing center, which would give care to all patients needing hospitalization within the area served. This hospital was opened on October 1, 1927.[20] The dedication was an important event and for the occasion Sir Leslie McKenzie and Lady

[19] "For the Last Quarter in the Field—the Three Centers," *The Quarterly Bulletin of the Kentucky Committee for Mothers and Babies, Inc.,* II, No. 2 (1926), pp. 3-4.

[20] "Laying the Corner Stones," *The Quarterly Bulletin of the Kentucky Committee for Mothers and Babies, Inc.,* III, No. 2 (1927), p. 3.

McKenzie came all the way from Scotland to Kentucky as guests of the service.[21]

This hospital was the only one in the entire area of three counties. The service had expanded to cover approximately 250 miles of the total 1,000 square mile territory, and had a staff of ten nurses; eight nurse-midwives, and two nurses who were not trained in midwifery.[22]

It was in 1928, three years after the initial meeting of the Kentucky Committee, that the members voted to change the title of the organization to the "Frontier Nursing Service."[23]

It is interesting to observe that when the nurses of the Kentucky Committee actually spent some years in caring for the families in the demonstration areas, they found that other services than midwifery and general public health nursing were so badly needed that their work could scarcely be fully satisfactory without the aid of a trained social worker and all types of professional medical and dental care. They found also that teaching the people to live healthy, resourceful lives was an important task for which, in that area, they alone were prepared.[24]

For the same reasons, the purpose of the Frontier Nursing Service was restated in 1931 to include phases of work that at first were not thought to be essential to the program. This revised statement of purpose has remained unchanged to the present and reads as follows:

> To safeguard the lives and health of mothers and children by providing and preparing trained nurse-midwives for rural areas in Kentucky and elsewhere, where there is inadequate medical service; to give skilled care to women in childbirth; to give nursing care to the sick of both sexes and all ages; to establish, own, maintain and operate hospitals, clinics, nursing centers, and midwifery training schools for graduate nurses; to educate the rural popula-

[21] "The Dedication," *The Quarterly Bulletin of the Frontier Nursing Service, Inc.,* IV, No. 2 (1928), pp. 1-3.

[22] "At Home," *Public Health Nursing,* XIX (1927), p. 607.

[23] "Announcement," *The Quarterly Bulletin of the Kentucky Committee for Mothers and Babies, Inc.,* III, No. 4 (1928), p. 2.

[24] *Ibid.*

tion in the laws of health, and parents in baby hygiene and child care; to provide expert social service; to obtain medical, dental and surgical services for those who need them at a price they can afford to pay, to ameliorate economic conditions inimical to health and growth, and to conduct research toward that end; to do any and all other things in any way incident to, or connected with, these objects, and, in pursuit of them, to cooperate with individuals and with organizations, whether private, state or federal; and through the fulfillment of these aims to advance the cause of health, social welfare and economic independence in rural districts with the help of their own leading citizens.[25]

Accounts of the work of the Frontier Nursing Service written by the nurse-midwives and by visitors to the area, give ample evidence of its success. In 1930 the Quarterly Bulletin reports:

We have extended our territory in still another direction. . . . This raises the territory we are covering to over 700 square miles. We are on the last lap of our first 1,000 mile demonstration area, and we are moving a little ahead of schedule time.[26]

With this further extension of the area, the ninth nursing center was opened. These centers bore names that were descriptive of their location: Hyden, Wendover, Beech Ford, Possum Bend, Red Bird River, Flat Creek, Brutus, Bowlingtown, and Beverly. Each one also was given a name indicating the donor. For reasons of brevity the former names are used more frequently. None of these centers were closer together than ten miles, and their districts extended into four counties.[27]

The annual reports bring out strikingly how the mountain people were responding to good maternity service and how the response was met. In 1927, the report gives the average number of nurse-midwives as three and three-fourths, the number of nursing centers as three, and the number of confinements attended during the year

[25] *The Quarterly Bulletin of the Frontier Nursing Service, Inc.,* VII, No. 2 (1931), p. 24.

[26] "The Summer's Work," *The Quarterly Bulletin of the Frontier Nursing Service, Inc.,* VI, No. 2 (1930), pp. 7-8.

[27] Betty Lester, "The Experiences of a Midwifery Supervisor in the Kentucky Hills," *The American Journal of Nursing,* XXXI (1931), p. 573.

as thirty-six. In 1929 there were fifteen nurse-midwives, six nursing centers, and one hundred and one confinements attended. In 1931 thirty-two nurse-midwives were employed, nine nursing centers were in operation and two hundred and forty-six deliveries conducted.

The depression struck the Frontier Nursing Service a heavy blow in 1931[28] that made it muster all its powers to give proper care to its thousands of families, one of the centers had to be closed because of an enforced personnel shortage. Funds were difficult to get. Many of the faithful contributors of former days were no longer able to lend support. It was only by the generosity and loyalty of a large proportion of the nurse-midwives who volunteered to keep on working, receiving only enough of their salaries to maintain themselves, and giving long hours of work with no vacations, that enabled the service to continue without more of its centers being closed. Many of the people were out of work and in order to help them Red Cross funds were obtained. Needed buildings were erected wherever possible to give some of them employment. Through all the hardships, however, the work continued and the number of confinements attended continued to mount a little each year in spite of the diminished number of staff members.[29]

About this time, too, other hardships came. In 1931 Mrs. Breckinridge fell from a horse and suffered a fractured vertebra which incapacitated her over a long period of time and has limited her activity ever since.[30] Several of the nurse-midwives met narrow escapes in fording swollen rivers between mountains while trying to reach a patient in need of care. The motto ,"if the father can come for the nurse, no matter what the weather, the nurse will always get to the mother," meant that the danger had to be risked.[31] On another occasion a staff member was bitten by a copperhead

[28] "Foreword," *The Quarterly Bulletin of the Frontier Nursing Service, Inc.*, VI, No. 4 (1931), p. 1.

[29] "Annual Report," *The Quarterly Bulletin of the Frontier Nursing Service, Inc.*, IX, No. 1 (1933), pp. 1-7.

[30] Mary Breckinridge, "Traveler and His Goat," *The Quarterly Bulletin of the Frontier Nursing Service, Inc.*, VII, No. 3 (1932), pp. 3-5.

[31] "Field Notes," *The Quarterly Bulletin of the Frontier Nursing Service, Inc.*, XI, No. 4 (1936), p. 21.

snake which resulted in a long illness despite the immediate administration of anti-venom serum.[32] Several illnesses also occurred
among the staff members, and one nurse-midwife, a native of
Ireland, died at the Hyden Hospital in spite of skilled medical and
nursing care.[33]

The spirit of trust in God that inspired so much heroism, kept
Mrs. Breckinridge hopeful. She once said when confronted with a
weighty problem, "one discovers that the Source of one's faith
never lets one down;"[34] and at another time:

> It has been our experience that when you do everything
> you can to meet a situation, God doesn't let you down. I
> have found that He often waits until you have done every-
> thing you can.[35]

Medical care and medical consultation services had been a problem since the earliest days. Doctors from Hazard and Lexington
had come periodically for a few days or a few weeks or on request
for consultation or surgery. In 1928 an arrangement was made
with the State Department for the services of one of its physicians.
This arrangement continued for three years when another period
of no local medical care was available.[36] In 1932 a resident physician
and obstetric specialist was employed at the Hyden Hospital who
acted as Medical Director for the entire service over a period of
almost twelve years when he left to enter the Army.[37] During vaca-
tion each year, there was always the difficulty of finding someone
to replace him. Somehow, it was managed, except for brief periods
when the nurses hoped nothing would happen with which they were
not prepared to cope and if it did they had to manage or send

[32] "Personals," *The Quarterly Bulletin of the Frontier Nursing Service,
Inc.,* VIII, No. 2 (1932), p. 17.

[33] *Ibid.,* pp. 16-17.

[34] Mary Breckinridge, "Rounds," *The Quarterly Bulletin of the Frontier
Nursing Service, Inc.,* V, No. 2 (1929), p. 11.

[35] "Field Notes," *The Quarterly Bulletin of the Frontier Nursing Service,
Inc.,* XIX, No. 1 (1943), p. 74.

[36] "Our First Medical Affiliation," *The Quarterly Bulletin of the Frontier
Nursing Service, Inc.,* VII, No. 3 (1932), p. 30.

[37] "Field Notes," *The Quarterly Bulletin of the Frontier Nursing Service,
Inc.,* XIX, No. 1 (1943), p. 73.

for a doctor many miles away. Since 1945 Henry S. Walters, M.D., has been resident physician and Medical Director.[38]

A succession of hardships has prevnted the Frontier Nursing Service from expanding as earlier it had hoped to do. The depression and then the war in Europe, both enforcing adjustments to a reduced number of staff members, came one after the other so rapidly that there was not time to regain the pre-depression momentum and further expand the work. The war hastened the inauguration of a nurse-midwifery training school, as will be recorded in chapter four, but at the same time America's involvement in the war and the continuous demand for nurses, claimed members of the Frontier Nursing Service staff just as from every other nursing group in the country. The present nursing staff has nineteen nurse-midwives. There are eight nursing centers; one of them is in connection with the Hyden Hospital.[39]

The Frontier Nursing Service was a local service as far as actual care of patients was concerned but it was also a service which, through its publicity, gave to the people of America some notion of what nurse-midwifery meant and of what the nurse-midwife was able to do. Soon after 1925 articles began to appear in nursing journals telling of the new work. In 1926 an editorial appeared in the April issue of the *American Journal of Nursing* entitled "Lack of Care of American Mothers," which brought out the high maternity and infant death rates in the United States as compared to these rates in other countries. Many other magazines, numerous newspapers, and a few books told the story of the nurse-midwives and their work for mothers and babies. Public addresses by prominent people who visited the Frontier Nursing Service and by Mrs. Breckinridge brought out the splendid work that was being done. In January 1927 one of the foremost nurses in the field of obstetrics at a conference of the State Directors in charge of the local administration of the Maternity and Infancy Act, brought out the need of a school for nurse-midwives in the United States

[38] "Field Workers," *The Quarterly Bulletin of the Frontier Nursing Service, Inc.*, XXI, No. 2 (1945), p. 102.

[39] "Field Workers," *The Quarterly Bulletin of the Frontier Nursing Service, Inc.*, XXI, No. 3 (1946), p. 74.

and lamented the fact that because there were no such schools in this country our nurses were obliged to go to England for this training. She expressed the belief that nurses who felt the need for being able to deliver normal cases and the right to do so would be glad to take the midwifery course if it were provided.[40] In 1928 Mary V. Pagaud, Superintendent of the Child Welfare Association in New Orleans, Louisiana, wrote "The Next Steps in Maternity Nursing," in which again nurse-midwifery was brought to the attention of the nursing profession.[41] The following year two articles were written by physicians who advocated the need for nurse-midwives. Carl Henry Davis, M.D., wrote:

> There is great need for graduate nurses who may qualify as midwives . . . . A nurse-midwife service, such as Mary Breckinridge has organized in the Kentucky mountains, if sufficiently developed might lead to a marked decrease in the maternal mortality rate of the United States.[42]

Benjamin P. Watson, M.D., of New York believed: "that the maternal mortality in this and in every other country would be very materially reduced if the practice of obstetrics were in the hands of thoroughly trained midwives working . . . . under the direction of properly trained doctors."[43]

All of this publicity and the part it played in influencing public opinion prepared the way for the first official American school of nurse-midwifery and for a broader field of work for American nurse-midwives.

---

[40] Carrie M. Hall, "Training the Obstetrical Nurse," *The American Journal of Nursing*, XXVII (1927), pp. 373-379.

[41] Public Health Nursing, XX (1928), pp. 622-625.

[42] "Obstetrics and Gynecology in General Practice," *The American Journal of Nursing*, XXIX (1929), p. 1443.

[43] "Can Our Methods of Obstetric Practice Be Improved?" *The American Journal of Nursing*, XXXI (1931), pp. 499-500.

CHAPTER III

THE FIRST RECOGNIZED AMERICAN SCHOOL OF NURSE-MIDWIFERY

In the first chapter of this study the early efforts of the Maternity Center Association in New York to open a school for nurse-midwifery were recorded. A sufficient number of physicians and nurses was not prepared to support such a movement in 1923, neither was the general public well enough acquainted with the need for good maternity care and the hazards resulting from inadequate or a complete lack of care to exert any influence by demanding well-prepared obstetric attendants. During the next ten years many factors combined to publicize not only the general obstetric conditions in this country but also the contrast between the mortality rates here and in other nations; the organization of educated, well-trained midwives to care for all mothers in countries where the maternal mortality rates were surprisingly low. The Frontier Nursing Service has "demonstrated conclusively"[1] that a system of nurse-midwifery worked well in remote areas of the United States just as it works well in Europe. The Maternity Center had reached thousands of nurses and expectant parents through its Institutes and classes for mothers and fathers.[2] Educated people were aware that maternity was safe only when proper safeguards were taken and that doctors and nurses were the guardians of these precautions. Public education for good maternity care was well under way.[3]

In 1931 the Maternity Center Association again attempted to organize a school for nurse-midwives in order to fill the need that it had recognized years before. Ralph Waldo Lobenstine, M.D., Chairman of the Medical Board since 1919,[4] had always been greatly interested in the possibilities of nurse-midwifery in the United States. Knowing that "if trained midwives are to succeed,

[1] George W. Kosmak, "The Trained Nurse and the Midwife," *The American Journal of Nursing*, XXXIV (1934), p. 423.

[2] *Maternity Center Association, 1918-1943*, pp. 56-57.

[3] "Laity and Social Workers," *Obstetric Education*. (Report of the Sub-Committee on Obstetric Teaching and Education, New York: The Century Co., 1933), p. 238.

[4] *Maternity Center Association, 1918-1923*, p. 64.

a means of bringing them under competent medical control must be devised,"[5] he, together with George W. Kosmak, M.D., Mrs. Mary Breckinridge, R.N., Benjamin P. Watson, M.D., Mrs. Marshall Field, James A. Harrar, M.D., Hazel Corbin, R.N., Lillian Hudson, R.N., and Linsly R. Williams, M.D., formed themselves into the Association for the Promotion and Standardization of Midwifery, Incorporated.[6] Together, they outlined the need for schools of nurse-midwifery and the principles of their control.

> These schools would graduate trained women who would recognize the importance of working under medical supervision and who, if later placed in supervisory positions in official health departments, would gradually be able to help bring about medical supervision of midwife practice.[7]

Ralph Waldo Lobenstine, M.D., had accepted a position on the staff of the New York Nursery and Child's Hospital on the condition that a school for nurse-midwives would be opened in connection with that institution. Plans were being completed for this project when Doctor Lobenstine died in 1931 and the Hospital dissolved its plans for the school. The other members of the Association for the Promotion and Standarization of Midwifery, however, were determined to open a school and decided to organize an entirely new maternity clinic to include a school for nurse-midwives as a memorial to Doctor Lobenstine, using the funds that had already been raised for this type of education.[8]

Without delay a suitable location was found at 274 W. 113th Street in the center of Harlem where the maternal mortality rate was very high and the average income, low. A physician was employed and Rose McNaught, a nurse-midwife, from the Frontier Nursing Service in Kentucky, came to New York. The physician, the nurse-midwife and Hattie Hemschemeyer, R.N., a public health

---

[5] *Ibid.,* p. 67.

[6] "A Training School for Nurse-Midwives Established," *The American Journal of Nursing,* XXXII (1932), p. 374.

[7] *Ibid.,* p. 374.

[8] *Maternity Center Association, 1918-1943, op. cit.,* p. 66.

nurse, formed the nursing staff of the Lobenstine Midwifery Clinic which opened in 1931.[9]

Very soon women began to register at the Clinic for care and by the following year a sufficient number had registered to warrant opening the school of nurse-midwifery. Definite plans included the following:

> .... The course in midwifery will cover a period of ten months. The first four months will include instruction, supervision, and practise in the general field of public health nursing with special emphasis on supervision. This work will be given under the supervision of the Department of Nursing Education, Teacher's College, Columbia University. The remaining six months in mid-wifery will include:
>
> (1) Lectures and demonstrations by obstetricians and nurse-midwives;
>
> (2) observation and instruction in cooperation with maternity hospitals;
>
> (3) observation of at least twenty-five labors and deliveries. The delivery of twenty-five women in their homes under the supervision of the resident obstetrician or the nurse-midwife.
>
> Preference will be given to applicants from states where the practice of midwifery is more common and where the individual applicant has the endorsement of the State Health Commissioner or Director of the Bureau of Child Hygiene.[10]

It is evident that the Clinic and School were well organized by the foresight of its Board of Directors and its policies clearly established from the outset. They have remained in the main unaltered to the present time. Hattie Hemschemeyer, Director of the School since 1934, said:[11] "A few basic principles were laid down: first: that all patients for this outdoor service would be carefully selected after a medical examination; second, that all abnormal patients would be referred to hospitals; third, that the functions to be per-

---

[9] Interview with Miss Hattie Hemschemeyer, June 1946.

[10] Hattie Hemschemeyer, "A Training School for Nurse-Midwives Established," *The American Journal of Nursing*, XXXII (1932), p. 374.

[11] Interview with Hattie Hemschemeyer, June 1946.

formed by the physician and the nurse-midwife should be clearly defined."[12] The primary purposes of the School and Clinic were stated as follows:

> 1. To study a field situation in which the care of the maternity patient is given by the obstetrician who delegates responsibility to the nurse-midwife. This study is being carried out to define methods and to study and test the results of the work, while maintaining throughout, a high grade of care to the patient.
> 2. To train a limited number of selected public health nurses who can find a place to use their training in the newer order; not to work as private practitioners or midwives, but as instructors and supervisors for the untrained midwives and for nurses with only an elementary deficient training in obstetric nursing.[13]

These objectives show two important differences from the system of nurse-midwifery practiced in some countries in Europe and Great Britain and followed by the Frontier Nursing Service in Kentucky. First, the nurse-midwife trained at the Lobenstine School would accept the responsibility of maternity care of normal patients delegated to her by the obstetrician after a complete physical examination had been given. And secondly, the nurse-midwife would not be a private practitioner as was the principle of work in Kentucky.[14] These differences made it necessary that nurse-midwives be employed only where medical care and medical consultation services are available. Their principle work would be in the field of supervision and instruction.

The obstetricians on the Medical Board of the School outlined the working plan and policies. "The principle of medical direction of the work was firmly established in the clinic and in the school."[15]

[12] Hattie Hemschemeyer, "Midwifery in the United States," *The American Journal of Nursing*, XXXIX (1939), p. 1186.

[13] *Ibid.*, p. 1186.

[14] Marion Laird, "Analysis of the First 1,081 Patients Cared For by the Lobenstine Clinic," Unpublished study, p. 1.

[15] Hattie Hemeschemeyer, "The Nurse-Midwife is Here to Stay," a paper presented at the Twenty-Fifth Anniversary Meeting of the Maternity Center Association, 1943, p. 4.

The large bulk of detailed work was delegated to the nurse-midwife staff with instructions to "consult when in doubt and to keep the medical personnel currently informed so they could decide what was to be done for each patient."[16]

In its early days the school met with continuous opposition[17] but those who believed in the need for nurse-midwives and wished to prove their value fought valiantly against all odds. George W. Kosmak, M.D., Chairman of the Medical Board was a strong supporter. In an article for the *American Journal of Nursing,* 1934, he said:

> The task that a nurse assumes as a midwife is one attended by personal sacrifice; her place in the obstetric scheme is not established as yet, it will take time and patience to work out this place, but I feel that until we have tried it out judgment must be reserved.[18]

During the same year he said: "This is a new and important field for the trained nurse who possesses the proper mental and physical qualifications for the task."[19]

Until 1934 Lobenstine Midwifery Clinic and School was conducted by the Association for the Promotion and Standardization of Midwifery, when, for its greater development and strength it was amalgamated with the Maternity Center Association and the Medical Board of the Maternity Center Association assumed the responsibility for directing the medical work of the Clinic.[20] As a result of this agreement, several members of the Medical Board resigned.[21] They did not believe in nurse-midwifery and did not want the Maternity Center Association to assume responsibility for such an educational program.

[16] *Ibid.*

[17] Hazel Corbin, "Doctors, Nurses and War," *Briefs,* VII (1942).

[18] George W. Kosmak, "The Trained Nurse and the Midwife," *The American Journal of Nursing,* XXXIV (1934), p. 423.

[19] George W. Kosmak, "Community Responsibilities for Safeguarding Motherhood," *Public Health Nursing* XXVI (1934), p. 298.

[20] *Life Begins,* p. 27, annual report of the Maternity Center Association, New York (1939).

[21] *Maternity Center Association, 1918-1943,* p. 26.

Opposition was confronted by the graduates of the school when they went into the various states to begin their work for the promotion of maternity care, and this opposition came from those with whom they had hoped to work: physicians and nurses.[22] This was a hardship that was borne not only by the nurse-midwife in the immediate situation but also by the faculty members of the school and those responsible for its existence. Hazel Corbin, Director of the Association reported that "they were looked upon with disdain, and there were some who were just waiting for them to make their first mistake."[23]

Despite the hardships that came, however, the school continued. In 1933 six nurses completed the midwifery course and from that year the school gradually gained momentum.[24] Records of maternity care won the esteem and admiration of the Medical Staff and Board. The first 1,712 patients registered at the Lobenstine Midwifery Clinic were delivered with a mortality rate of 1.8 per 1,000 live births, as compared to a rate of 7.5 in the same area for all mothers; and a still birth rate of 30 per 1,000 live births, as compared with 65.5 among all the births of the same district. This was a reduction comparable to that achieved by the Frontier Nursing Service nurse-midwives, and by the Chicago Maternity Center with its staff of physicians.[25]

The number of students graduated each year ranged from five to eleven until 1942 when the practice field was enlarged by the acquisition of the John E. Berwind Maternity Clinic at 127 East 103rd Street. This Clinic, previously used by medical students of the Cornell Medical School and New York Lying-in Hospital, housed in a large building which was centrally located, provided ample room for the teaching and administrative offices of the school, a well-equipped modern maternity clinic, and a large group of patients.

The Berwind Branch, as this newly acquired clinic was called,

---

[22] Hazel Corbin, "Doctors, Nurses and War," *Briefs,* VII (1942).

[23] *Ibid.*

[24] Analysis of *Student Records* sent by Miss Hemschemeyer.

[25] *Public Health Nursing in Obstetrics,* Part I, rev. (Maternity Center Association, New York, 1941), pp. 14-15.

became the headquarters for the School of Nurse-Midwifery and the former building was retained as a clinic and provided sleeping quarters for some of the students. During 1943 three classes of students were admitted and nineteen students were graduated. Since that time the enrollment has fluctuated only slightly and each year three classes are admitted.[26]

Most of the students who have attended the nurse-midwifery schools have received scholarships either from the Maternity Center Association, from Federal or State funds, from private agencies and individuals or a combination of these.[27]

The service runs with a medical executive committee, a medical director, two associate medical directors, and seven full time nurse-midwives. Three classes of students are admitted each year with six nurses in each class. The entrance requirements as stated in the school bulletin, specify that the applicant must have graduated from an accredited school of nursing and be eligible for college matriculation; be between twenty-five and forty years of age, and have had at least two years of professional experience. Nurses in the field of public health nursing must have had one year of experience in public health under supervision; those from institutions are allowed to substitute for this year of public health experience a year's work in teaching and supervision under supervision in a hospital. The school prefers that students be sponsored by agencies that will employ them when they have completed the course.[28]

The midwifery course itself, as described in the latest school bulletin consists of "1,100 hours of work—including 185 hours of lectures and 100 tutorial hours; also work in the prenatal and postnatal clinics, field work in the homes of the patients, with each student delivering a minimum of twenty patients, under expert supervision."[29] The school charges a tuition of one hundred and fifty dollars. This is the only fee charged. All travel expenses of

[26] Analysis of *Students Records, op. cit.*

[27] *Ibid.*

[28] Interview with Hattie Hemschemeyer, June 1946.

[29] *Announcement of the School of Nurse-Midwifery,* Maternity Center Association, New York, p. 7.

students, incurred through care of patients are paid by the school. For several years a forty-four hour week has been in use.

Although the initial plan was for a ten month course, this was found not to be fully satisfactory and was not continued; students are not required to attend Columbia University. However, the affiliation is still effective and college credits are granted to properly qualified students for the six-months midwifery course.

During the course, classes are given in the following subjects:

1. The Science and Art of Obstetrics, 45 hours.
2. Public Health Nursing in Obstetrics, 45 hours.
3. Midwifery Techniques, 50 hours.
4. Administration and Supervision of Maternal Health and Nurse-Midwife Services, 30 hours.
5. Teaching the Public About Maternity, 15 hours.

Tutorial hours are estimated at from 80 to 100 hours. This includes "conferences with teaching staff on each phase of the work—labor call, clinic or field visits, records, bags, observations, techniques and the perfection of skills."[30] Examinations in each subject are given at the end of each two months with an oral examination by a member of the medical board at the completion of the six month course.[31]

The school announcement describes the course in nurse-midwifery and explains the conviction of Maternity Center Association regarding it as follows:

> A course in nurse-midwifery is an intensive course in the practical art and science of obstetrics. It helps the nurse to a better understanding of maternity in relation to family living. It is the conviction of the Maternity Center Association that nurses who teach expectant parents, act as maternity and child health consultants to, or supervisors of public health nurses, supervise maternity departments in hospitals, or teach obstetrics in schools of nursing should have no less obstetric preparation that that given in a nurse-midwifery course.[32]

[30] *Ibid.*, p. 16.
[31] *Ibid.*
[32] *Ibid.*, p. 19.

Between 1932 and June 1946 the School has graduated 125 nurse-midwives who are located in thirteen foreign countries and thirty states and the District of Columbia. Of these nurse-midwives 62.4 percent have obtained either the Master's or Baccalaureate degree. Each year more of the students on coming to the school have completed college. At the present time, June 1946, there are twelve students enrolled and all but one holds a Baccalaureate degree and two hold the Master's degree.[33]

The thirteen years of experience with the midwifery school and with the nurse-midwives who have gone to work in every part of the world, has convinced the Officers of the Maternity Center Association that the methods used by its School and Clinic are safe and practical. The experience has also proved that the nurse-midwife and the obstetrician can work together, when proper relationships are developed, to give a community maternal and infant care that is adequate, acceptable, and scientific.

[33] Analysis of *Students Records.*

CHAPTER IV

OTHER SCHOOLS OF NURSE-MIDWIFERY IN THE UNITED STATES

Altogether six schools have been established for the preparation of nurse-midwives. One of them, the Lobenstine Midwifery School, we have already discussed in chapter three. A seventh school, Preston Retreat, although not originally established for nurse-midwifery, has subsequently admitted graduate nurses to the school and upon completing the course, conferred upon them a certificate of midwifery.[1]

These seven schools have graduated approximately 225 nurse-midwives.

The Manhattan Midwifery School

The very first school for nurse-midwifery to be established in the United States, although it was not officially recognized, was the Manhattan Midwifery School founded in 1928 in connection with the Manhattan Maternity and Dispensary in New York. Very little information could be obtained by the writer regarding this school. *Public Health Nursing,* December 1928, printed in its "News Notes" an announcement that Mary M. Richardson, the former Instructor of Public Health Nursing at the Providence District Nursing Association had taken the midwifery course in England and after having studied the various types of midwifery schools in several European countries had returned to become Director of Nurses at the Manhattan Maternity and Dispensary in New York, and added: "A course in midwifery is now being offered at the Manhattan Maternity to public health nurses and nurses contemplating missionary work."[2]

In September of the same year the *Quarterly Bulletin of the Frontier Nursing Service* gave in its "Staff Notes" the following announcements: "Miss Katherine Stiles and Miss Doris Beaumont, who are the first graduates of the new course in midwifery at the Manhattan Maternity in New York City, arrived early in Sep-

[1] Personal letter from Stella Mummert, Superintendent of Preston Retreat Hospital, June 1946.

[2] *News Notes* XX (1928), p. 612.

tember . . . ."[3] The announcement goes on to say that the course
was six months in length.

It was not possible to determine the year this school closed. All
printed articles speak of the Lobenstine Midwifery School as the
first in the United States. Therefore, the Manhattan Midwifery
School evidently had been closed by 1932. No other information
was available.

Preston Retreat

The Preston Retreat, School of Midwifery was mentioned in
Chapter I as one of the two well-known schools for midwives that
existed over a fairly long period of time. This school was opened
in 1923 in Philadelphia, and about ten years later, its faculty, recognizing the diminished need for native midwives in that city, shifted
its emphasis to the training of graduate nurses. The school is conducted in a fifty-bed all-maternity, free hospital which was built
and endowed a century ago (1836) for the care of indigent married
mothers in Philadelphia. A nurse-midwife, Stella Mummert, is
superintendent of the Hospital and in charge of the nursing. She
and her assistant nurse-midwife do all the normal deliveries. Between 1933 and 1942, four graduate professional registered nurses
completed the midwifery course. Two college women took the course
during the time who, afterwards became nurses.[4]

Instruction in the school is given by an obstetrician, and a nurse-
midwife. It includes thirty-three hours of formal classroom teaching.
Students conduct from thirty to forty deliveries under the supervision of the nurse-midwife. All deliveries are conducted in the
hospital. It is the only school that has offered a midwifery course
with all student experience in a hospital.[5]

The Frontier Graduate School of Midwifery

Early in its program the Frontier Nursing Service saw the possibility of using its maternity patients as a laboratory for student

---

[3] *The Quarterly Bulletin of the Frontier Nursing Service, Inc.,* IV, No. 2
(1928), p. 12.

[4] Letters from Stella Mummert dated June 24 and July 3, 1946.

[5] *Ibid.*

nurse-midwives. *The Quarterly Bulletin of the Frontier Nursing Service* gives clue to this aspiration at various times after 1928. The restated aims of the Service also indicated this idea. The Bulletin reads: the staff is "eager to get on with the training end" to use the vast laboratory as a field of practice.[6] It is interesting to observe that the plan was to work in cooperation with a University where students could obtain the necessary theoretical part of the midwifery course and then come to the mountains for the actual practice.[7]

During the early part of 1936 two Indian nurses spent one year at the Frontier Nursing Service in preparation for the work that would confront them when they returned to their own people in the Southwest. A survey of the need for nurse-midwifery had been done by Mary B. Willeford, R.N., Assistant Director of the Frontier Nursing Service, at the request of the Indian Bureau, to determine the distribution of experience that would best fill the needs of these nurses.[8] During the year nineteen lectures were given by the Medical Director of the service, eleven classroom periods were spent with the Hospital nurse-midwife, and their midwifery experience was directed by Dorothy Buck, Midwifery Supervisor. The entire program was arranged and supervised by Miss Willeford. As a result of this experience the Bulletin stated: "Our experience with these students has shown us that we cannot do a complete and thorough piece of work with others until we have our midwifery school affiliated with the University of Kentucky."[9]

In 1939 the large majority of the nurse-midwives employed by the Frontier Nursing Service were citizens of England. The original plan was to have a nursing staff consisting of an equal

[6] "A National Demonstration," *The Quarterly Bulletin of the Frontier Nursing Service, Inc.*, XI, No. 4 (1936), p. 6.

[7] Mary B. Willeford, "Organization and Supervision of the Fieldwork of the Frontier Nursing Service, Inc." *The Quarterly Bulletin of the Frontier Nursing Service, Inc.*, X (1935), p. 22.

[8] Mary B. Willeford and Bland Morrow, "Study of Certain Indian Reservations of the Southwest," *The Quarterly Bulletin of the Frontier Nursing Service, Inc.*, XI, No. 3 (1936), pp. 21-23.

[9] "Indian Nurses," *The Quarterly Bulletin of the Frontier Nursing Service, Inc.*, XI, No. 3 (1936), pp. 19-20.

number of British and American nurse-midwives.[10] In the early years scholarships were given to American nurses who wished to study midwifery and this balance was maintained until the depression struck and the midwifery course in England was lengthened to one year. This made further scholarships seem impractical and as a result by September 1939, eighteen of the twenty-three nurse-midwives on the staff were British. The war had not been reckoned with and there had seemed no fear of a shortage of personnel. The outbreak of war in England was a plea to British citizens to stand faithful and these nurses felt it their duty to return, not only to give their nursing service but for the comfort and support of their families. The decrease in staff members began immediately and since the service employed no extra staff members, there was a corresponding shortage. Something had to be done quickly in order to keep the nursing centers open and take care of mothers who were registered for confinement under the care of the nurse-midwives.[11]

Since there was only one school existent in the United States and its program was limited and they could take only two students from Kentucky, the only possible solution was to provide training within the service. In two months a program had been organized and a class of two students was admitted.[12]

The opening of the School necessitated reorganization within the service in order to divide the generalized program from the maternity work. The Midwifery was put into the care of the training school and the other nursing was done by a graduate non-midwife staff nurse.[13] An announcement of the school appeared in the *American Journal of Nursing* in March, 1940:

> The Frontier Nursing Service has recently launched a program to train American graduate nurses in midwifery, to meet the demand for such nurses in its own and other rural health services. Two nurses, formerly in the Serv-

---

[10] Dorothy Buck, "The Nurses on Horseback Ride On," *The American Journal of Nursing*, XL (1940), p. 993.

[11] *Ibid.*, p. 993.

[12] *Ibid.*

[13] *Ibid.*

ices's Hospital at Hyden, Kentucky, are now preparing for "field-service" under the direction of graduate nurse-midwives and obstetricians. They will be examined for certification at the end of their course.[14]

In the beginning the course was four months but plans were made to extend it to six months as soon as the urgent demand for staff members would be alleviated. The school followed the general plan required by the Central Midwives Board. Both hospital and district cases were included in the teaching and experience of the students. Scholarships were offered, to cover tuition and living expenses, by the Service. Only graduate, registered nurses were admitted to the course and these nurses were required to have had some experience in district nursing, and show aptitude for the work. The plan was to have applicants work in some capacity not requiring midwifery for a time before admitting them to the midwifery course. This served as a basis of selection and gave some assurance that the nurse was genuinely interested and suitable for midwifery.[15]

The program of studies as given in the school bulletin includes thirty-two lectures by the Medical Director and thirty-six by the Nurse-Midwife Instructor. No other information is given.

At the completion of the course, oral and written examinations were given by two physicians from the State Board of Health of Kentucky, and diplomas were issued by the Frontier Nursing Service.[16] Graduates of the school are entitled to put the initials C.M. after their names to designate that they are Certified Midwives. The Director of the State Board of Health of Kentucky did not approve the S.C.M. (State Certified Midwife) as used in Great Britain because Kentucky is not a State but a Commonwealth.[17]

During 1940 the Executive Committee of the organization

[14] "Causes for Nurse-Midwives," *The American Journal of Nursing,* XL (1940), p. 335.

[15] Dorothy Buck, "The Nurses on Horseback Ride On," *The American Journal of Nursing,* XL (1940), p. 994.

[16] "Field Notes," *The Quarterly Bulletin of the Frontier Nursing Service, Inc.,* XVI, No. 1 (1940), p. 68.

[17] "Field Workers," *The Quarterly Bulletin of the Frontier Nursing Service, Inc.,* XVIII, No. 1 (1942), p. 74.

adopted the title of Frontier Graduate School of Midwifery for its new school and Dorothy F. Buck, R.N., S.C.M., M.A., was appointed the first Dean. Eva Gilbert, R.N., S.C.M., M.A., a staff member, was appointed Instructor of Midwifery.[18] On December 1, 1940, when the third class of three students was admitted, the course was lengthened to six months.[19]

In the fall of 1941 a class of four was admitted. The number of students admitted at one time remained the same until 1944. During that year five students were admitted. In the fall of 1945, the class was increased to six members. During this year, if the present class of six complete the course, twelve students will have been given diplomas in nurse-midwifery. Eight of the forty-two graduates of the Frontier Graduate School of Midwifery are missionaries.[20]

Since the School opened, the staff of the Frontier Nursing Service has been made up largely of its own graduates.[21]

Tuskegee School of Nurse-Midwifery

Recognizing the need for colored nurse-midwives in the South, the Alabama State Department of Health sent two colored nurses to the School for Nurse-Midwifery in New York preparatory to opening a school in that State. Following their midwifery course, these nurses returned to the Macon County Health Department and in collaboration with the physicians began a direct midwifery service. On September 15, 1941, the Tuskegee School of Nurse-Midwifery was opened.[22] Margaret Thomas, R.N., C.N.M., M.A., a member of the staff of the Maternity Center Association in New York, was the first Director of the school. It was established as a joint project of the Tuskegee Institute and the Alabama State Department of Health. Funds to assist in financing the school were

[18] "Personnel." *The Quarterly Bulletin of the Frontier Nursing Service, Inc.*, XVI, No. 3 (1941), p. 74.

[19] "The Frontier Graduate School of Midwifery," *The Quarterly Bulletin of the Frontier Nursing Service, Inc.*, XVII, No. 1 (1941), p. 13.

[20] Letter of Dorothy Buck dated July 1946.

[21] Analysis of the "Field Workers" as given in each issue of *The Quarterly Bulletin of the Frontier Nursing Service, Inc.*

[22] Margaret Thomas, "Social Priority No. 1: Mothers and Babies," *Public Health Nursing* XXXIV (1942), p. 442.

allotted by the Children's Bureau to be administered by the Health Officer.[23]

The 1943 Report of the Alabama Health Department records the early planning as following:

> The groundwork for the Tuskegee Nurse-Midwife School was laid on August 1, 1939, when nurse-midwifery service was offered in Beats Four and Five in Macon County. At the same time hospitalization for problem maternity cases and sick infants was provided by the John A. Andrew Memorial Hospital in Tuskegee. A Negro obstetrician was attached to the Macon County Health Department to serve as clinician in the maternity clinics of the County and attend hospital deliveries of indigent cases. The service was further extended by the addition of three nurse-midwives in March, 1941.[24]

After the school was under way Margaret Thomas returned to Maternity Center and Carrington Owen, a ▉▉▉▉ nurse-midwife who had taken midwifery in New York, became the second Director of the Tuskegee school. Thirteen Negro nurses had been graduated by 1943. During that same year several of the five staff members left and it was necessary to discontinue the school until the fall of that year when Miss Thomas returned to Tuskegee, resumed the Directorship, and the school was opened with a class of two students. At the same time the Children's Bureau agreed to provide a "basic budget for the Tuskegee Nurse-Midwife Training School, thereby relieving Alabama of financial responsibility,"[25] because it recognized the need for colored nurse-midwives throughout the Southern States and felt that this school could provide them. Miss Thomas remained for about one year.

However, because of difficulties that were not determined by this study, the school has now been closed for complete reorganization.[26]

---

[23] Letter from Ruth Doran of the U. S. Children's Bureau dated July 1, 1946.

[24] Mimeographed copy of section from 1943 report: "Tuskegee Nurse-Midwife Training School." Sent to me by Pearl Barclay, Director of the Division of Public Health Nursing, Montgomery, Ala.

[25] *Ibid.*

[26] Letter from Ruth Doran, July 1, 1946.

It was impossible to determine the total number of nurses who had completed the course prior to its closing.

> Several of the graduates are now employed in hospitals in the Obstetric Department as instructors or supervisors. In Florida, Alabama, Maryland, and Arkansas, several of the graduates are employed by the State Department of Health in the Maternal and Child Health programs.[27]

Flint Goodridge School of Nurse-Midwifery

In 1942 a school for nurse-midwifery was opened in New Orleans, Louisiana, in connection with the Flint Goodridge Hospital and Dillard University. It was at least partially financed by funds obtained from the Federal Children's Bureau. Kate Hyder, R.N., C.N.M., M.A., a graduate of the School for Nurse-Midwives in New York, was in charge. It remained open one year from 1942 to August 1943. The project was abandoned after two nurses completed the course. These nurse-midwives are employed by the Health Departments in Louisiana and Mississippi respectively.[28]

Catholic Maternity Institute, School for Nurse-Midwifery

After the groundwork had been planned by the Archbishop of Santa Fe, the New Mexico State Department of Health, and the U. S. Children's Bureau, for a complete maternity service for the Spanish-speaking population of the territory surrounding Santa Fe, the Medical Mission Sisters from Philadelphia, Pennsylvania, agreed to provide the service and in connection with it to open a school for nurse-midwives.

In November 1943 two Sisters, Sister M. Helen Herb and Sister M. Theophane Shoemaker, both nurse-midwives, who had trained at the Maternity Center Association School for Nurse-Midwifery in New York, went to Santa Fe and began the midwifery work through the prenatal service which already existed at the Catholic Clinic. This Clinic was owned by the Archdiocese and had been built in 1936. For ten months the Sisters worked at this general clinic and at the same time gave special attention to the maternity

[27] *Ibid.*
[28] Letter from Ruth Doran.

service. The obstetrician who had conducted the clinics had also been delivering the poor patients in their homes because there were no other facilities available except the indigenous midwives. Within two months she persuaded the Sisters to assume the responsibility for these confinements and by the first of February they were prepared to do so. During the same period they assisted the doctor with the care of her private patients during confinement in their homes. This ten months at the Catholic Clinic served as an excellent introduction to the local population, gave time for planned organization, and paved the way for the opening of the Catholic Maternity Institute in August, 1944.

During the ten months at the Catholic Clinic the number of patients registered for maternity care had grown tremendously and sixty-three deliveries had been conducted by the Sisters.[29] In early August, 1944, the third Sister nurse-midwife came to Santa Fe and one other Sister, a dietician, arrived. On August 15, the official opening of the Catholic Maternity Institute took place. The purpose of the Institute as stated in its Charter of Incorporation is:

> a. Giving direct maternity service by nurse-midwives under the medical direction of a qualified physician in areas where this service is needed.
> b. Conducting a school of nurse-midwifery; . . . .
> c. Promoting maternal and infant health as opportunity and need may present.[30]

On September 1, 1944 the School for Nurse-Midwifery was officially opened but students were not admitted until February 1, 1945. The first six months were spent in organizing the program. Sister M. Theophane Shoemaker, R.N., B.S., C.N.M., was appointed Director of the Institute and Sister M. Michael Waters, R.N., B.S., C.N.M., Assistant Director. From the very beginning it had been planned that the school should be affiliated with the School of Nursing Education of the Catholic University of America, Washington, D. C. When all preliminary work had been completed the University sent a faculty member to evaluate the program.

[29] Statistical Report, September 1, 1944.

[30] Charter of Incorporation. Catholic Maternity Institute, Santa Fe, New Mexico, August 4, 1945.

Three months later the school received its Certificate of Affiliation with the Catholic University which promised official recognition of credits given by the School to its students.[31]

One of the recommendations given by the Catholic University was that the Director of the School "should be given a leave of absence. . . . for advanced study in Nursing Education to include Organization and Administration."[32] In order to properly equip the faculty early in the program it was decided that the school year 1945-46 should be used for this purpose.

During 1944, the nurse-midwives conducted 103 deliveries; in 1945, 144; and during the first six months of 1946, there were 86.

The policy of the Institute is to admit only those patients who live within a thirty mile radius of Santa Fe and near roads that can be traveled by car. It has been found that patients if well instructed, will call sufficiently early in labor to enable the nurse to arrive even though it may take as much as an hour from the time the call is received. All deliveries are conducted in the homes.

The faculty of the School consists of three full-time nurse-midwives, one obstetrician who attends two clinics each week and is on call at all times for consultation, and a pediatrician who teaches, acts as a consultant and is responsible for all infants who are hospitalized. There are four part-time lecturers.

An agreement has been made with St. Vincent's Hospital in Santa Fe to admit all patients registered by the nurse-midwives needing hospitalization. The State Department of Health and the Federal Children's Bureau, or the Department of Public Welfare, have in the majority of instances, paid the hospital fee. Medical care is given by the Obstetrician or Pediatrician of the Institute Staff.

The nurse-midwives have a list of Standing Orders made up by the Obstetrician covering ordinary needs. For special orders the physician is consulted. The obstetrician is called by the nurse-midwife to any confinements that are abnormal or at other times when the condition of the patient warrants it. The working rela-

[31] Dr. Roy J. Defarrari, Secretary-General, Chairman of the Committee on Affiliation.

[32] "Data Presented for Consideration of the Committee on Affiliation and Extension."

tions with the physician are very similar to those at the Maternity Center in New York.

On February 1, 1945, the first class of two students were admitted to the School and completed the course on August 5, 1945. One of them is now employed by the New Mexico State Department of Health for a direct nurse-midwife delivery service north of Santa Fe, and the other is Supervisor and Instructor in the maternity department of the San Jose Hospital in California.

The program of studies is as follows:

> Midwifery Techniques and Procedures, 60 hours.
> The Art and Science of Obstetrics, 45 hours.
> Public Health Nursing in Maternal and Child Health, 30 hours.
> Mothers' Classes, 15 hours.

Field work requires about 500 hours and approximately the same amount of time is allowed for clinics and related work and study. Students are required to report at the school five days before regular classes begin for an orientation period. The school has been financed by the Society of Catholic Medical Missionaries supported by funds from the Federal Children's Bureau obtained through the New Mexico State Department of Health.

Summary of Qualifications and Tuition

Although there has been no authoritative minimum standards set up to guide the schools in the selection of students or in their requirements, each school has set up its own schedule. An analysis of the school bulletins reveals that these are very similar. All require that applicants be high-school graduates, have completed the basic nursing course in an accredited hospital and be in good health. The schools in New Mexico, New York, and Tuskegee require some experience in public health nursing and specify an age requirement of 25-40 years. The schools in New York and New Mexico require that applicants have two years of professional experience before being admitted to the school. The Tuskegee school requires only one year but specifies that it must be in the field of public health. The other schools have no requirements of professional experience beyond the basic nursing course.

Tuitions vary greatly among the schools, as is shown in Table 1.

TABLE 1.

TUITION CHARGED BY NURSE-MIDWIFERY SCHOOLS

Location of School	Tuition
Kentucky	$560.00
New Mexico	150.00
New York	150.00
Philadelphia	000.00
Tuskegee (closed temporarily)	200.00

The school in Tuskegee has extra fees amounting to $183.50. Extra fees are not charged by the other schools with the exception of a maintenance fee in the Kentucky school. The other schools make no provision for maintenance.

Programs of study are not given in all the school bulletins in sufficient detail to allow comparison. Whatever information that the bulletins of the individual schools give, has been incorporated in the account of each school.

All courses are six months in length.

CHAPTER V

Nurse-Midwifery Activities in the United States

The preceeding chapters presented the larger nurse-midwifery centers in the United States where new students are trained in the profession and the activities of nurse-midwives in these centers. An effort was made to collect data concerning other nurse-midwives who are employed by the Health Departments in the various states. It was not possible in the scope of this study to discover how many nurse-midwives are employed by other agencies and institutions.

The Directors were asked for information regarding the number of nurse-midwives employed by the respective states and the types of positions they filled; and whether or not the state had any provision for licensing nurse-midwives. Replies were received from every Director without exception. (See Table 2 for details.)

An analysis of the information received shows that thirty-three states have no nurse-midwives employed. Four of these states have employed nurse-midwives in the past but did not have any on their staffs at the present time. One state did not specify whether or not nurse-midwives were employed. The remaining fifteen states have a total of forty nurse-midwives employed at the present time. These nurses are employed in the following capacities: consultants, those giving a direct delivery service, supervisors of indigenous midwives, and general staff nurses.

Eight states have nurse-midwives employed as consultants (general or in maternal and child health). These states are Arkansas, the District of Columbia, Louisiana, Maryland, Massachusetts, Missouri, South Carolina, and Vermont. A few years ago a nurse-midwife was employed as the consultant nurse in Maine but she is no longer there. Nebraska has sent its consultant on maternal and infant health to the School of Nurse-Midwifery Maternity Center Association and she will return to the state as soon as she has completed the course.

TABLE 2.
NURSE-MIDWIVES EMPLOYED BY THE STATE HEALTH DEPARTMENTS

State	No. of Nurse-Midwives	Type of Position				
		Consultant	General Staff	Midwife Superv'n	Direct Service	Other
Alabama	3	..	..	..	..	3
Arizona	0	..	..	..	..	..
Arkansas	2	1	..	1	..	..
California	3	..	3	..	..	..
Colorado	0	..	..	..	..	..
Connecticut	0	..	..	..	..	..
Delaware	0	..	..	..	..	..
Dist. of Col.	1	1	..	..	..	..
Florida	6	..	..	6	..	..
Georgia	1	..	1	..	..	..
Illinois	0	..	..	..	..	..
Indiana	0	..	..	..	..	..
Iowa	0	..	..	..	..	..
Idaho	0	..	..	..	..	..
Kansas	0	..	..	..	..	..
Kentucky	1	..	..	..	..	1
Louisiana	2	1	..	1	..	..
Maine	0	..	..	..	..	..
Maryland	8	1	..	6	..	1
Massachusetts	1	1	..	..	..	..
Michigan	0	..	..	..	..	..
Minnesota	0	..	..	..	..	..
Mississippi	1	..	..	1	..	..
Missouri	1	1	..	..	..	..
Montana	0	..	..	..	..	..
Nevada	0	..	..	..	..	..
N. Dakota	0	..	..	..	..	..
Nebraska	0	..	..	..	..	..
New Hampshire	0	..	..	..	..	..
New Jersey	0	..	..	..	..	..
New Mexico	5	..	2	..	3	..
New York	0	..	..	..	..	..
N. Carolina	0	..	..	..	..	..
Ohio	0	..	..	..	..	..
Oklahoma	0	..	..	..	..	..
Oregon	0	..	..	..	..	..
Pennsylvania	?	..	..	..	..	..
Rhode Island	0	..	..	..	..	..
S. Carolina	4	1	2*	2*	3*	..
S. Dakota	0	..	..	..	..	..
Tennessee	0	..	..	..	..	..
Texas	0	..	..	..	..	..
Utah	0	..	..	..	..	..
Virginia	0	..	..	..	..	..
Washington	0	..	..	..	..	..
W. Virginia	0	..	..	..	..	..
Wisconsin	0	..	..	..	..	..
Wyoming	0	..	..	..	..	..
Vermont	1	1	..	..	..	..
TOTAL	40	8	8	17	6	5

* Represents a divided program.

Only two states, New Mexico and South Carolina, have nurse-midwives employed for direct maternity service including care of confinements. New Mexico has two nurse-midwives at El Rito, a small village about fifty miles north of Santa Fe, where they have a maternity clinic and carry a full midwifery program. An obstetrician from Santa Fe attends regular clinics and gives every patient a complete physical examination soon after she registers for care, and acts as a medical director and consultant to the nurse-midwives. There is a second clinic at Abuiqui, sixteen miles away, where regular clinics are held also and these same nurse-midwives cover both districts for delivery service. The program was established in April 1945 and up to June 1, 1946, twenty-three patients had been delivered by the nurses. At the present time, one of the nurses is on a two months' leave of absence to complete her college work. A third nurse-midwife is employed by the New Mexico State Department of Health and participates in the direct delivery service at the Catholic Maternity Institute which was discussed in a previous chapter.

The second state that has nurse-midwives employed in a direct delivery service is South Carolina. Three nurses are working in this capacity. Rosa Clark, R.N., C.M., is located in a mountainous section of Oconee County and runs a complete program with clinics, home visits, and delivery service. She has conducted 152 confinements during the two years she has been there. The other two nurse-midwives carry a combined program helping the indigenous midwives with their deliveries, teaching their classes, assisting at prenatal clinics, and doing deliveries when patients are referred by either physicians or midwives.

Ten states have launched programs for nurse-midwife supervision of native midwives since 1935. None had been attempted before that time. Nurse-midwives so employed work with these untrained women in an effort to teach them the rudiments of cleanliness, to have patients register for medical care early in pregnancy, to recognize abnormalities, and to call for assistance when a confinement seems abnormal. Four of these ten states have wholly abandoned the programs and two of the other states have abandoned individual county programs from time to time.

The states that have abandoned their programs wholly or in part did not all specify the reasons that led to their discontinuance. The specific reasons enumerated were the following: 1. A shortage of available nurse-midwives; 2. Lack of funds; 3. Lack of evidence of sufficient improvement in the work of the indigenous midwives to warrant the cost. It is very evident that problems have been encountered by the various counties in attempting to conduct this type of program. In several states one county after another has attempted to establish such a program but after some months or a few years the projects were abandoned for reasons that were inadequately stated or, in many cases, not mentioned at all. In one state such a program has been started in nine counties and five of the nine have discontinued them. The letter received from the office of the Nursing Director gave the following explanation: "Our programs are being evaluated . . . . We believe that probably some of our programs were started too hastily and for this reason did not survive."

Another state that initiated the same type of program in five counties about four years ago has discontinued the programs in all counties and summarized the results in its annual report as follows: "The results can be briefly summarized by stating that no concrete evidence exists to warrant the conclusion that lay midwives have in any way improved sufficiently to justify the cost of the service."

The names of the six states that are continuing their supervision programs and the number of nurses employed for this purpose are as follows: Arkansas, 1; Florida, 6; Louisiana, 1; Maryland, 6; Mississippi, 1; and South Carolina, 2 who devote part time to this work.

The oldest and most extensive of these nurse-midwife supervision programs for indigenous midwives, is conducted by the Maryland State Department of Health. It was initiated by Elizabeth Ferguson, R.N., C.N.M., in 1936 in St. Charles County. For five years accurate records were kept in an effort to determine what might be done for mothers and children of limited means, with the added help of a nurse-midwife.[1] During these years the number of women in the area attending prenatal clinics increased from eighty-one in

---

[1] Elizabeth Ferguson, R.N., "Nurses-Midwives Serve a Rural County," reprinted from *Public Health Nursing*, April 1943.

1936 to 200 in 1940 despite a slight drop in the total number of births; 439 in 1936 and 411 in 1940.

Of the 879 patients examined in the clinics there was only one maternal death and 89 percent of the deliveries were spontaneous. There were twenty-six stillborn infants and twenty-two neonatal deaths over the five year period. Miss Ferguson accredited these remarkably low figures to the intensive follow-up work by the nurses and the cooperation of the mothers to call for the nurse at the first sign of illness.[2] This program was subsequently closed.

In 1937 another program was started by the Maryland State Department of Health which was very similar to that in Charles County but it has continued to the present time and is still very active. Martha Solotar, R.N., C.N.M., who graduated from the School of Nurse-Midwifery in New York, May 1937, went to Salisbury, Maryland, and it is largely through her personal effort that the work has succeeded so well. She gives a limited amount of her time to direct delivery service but most of it is spent in the clinics, in teaching and supervising indigenous midwives and in home visiting. Four other counties have nurse-midwives employed at the present time.

The Kentucky State Department of Health employs one nurse-midwife at the Maternity Hospital at Oneida. This nurse acts as general supervisor and does head nurse duties.

Four states have nurse-midwives employed as general staff nurses. These states and the number of nurse-midwives employed in this capacity are: California, 3; Georgia, 1; New Mexico, 2; and South Carolina has two nurse-midwives who devote part of their time to a generalized program.

Besides the specific data regarding the nurse-midwives employed by the Health Departments of the various states, there are a few other items of information regarding the employment of nurse-midwives which were revealed by this study and are of interest.

The United States Children's Bureau has on its staff four nurse-midwives, all of whom are graduates of the Maternity Center Association's School of Nurse-Midwifery in New York. They are Ruth Doran, Public Health Nursing Consultant; Caroline Russell,

[2] *Ibid.*

Inter-American Unit; Lalla Mary Goggans, Regional Nursing Consultant, Dallas, Texas; Margaret Thomas, Regional Nursing Consultant, San Francisco, California.

Analysis of data also showed that there are at least five nurse-midwives employed on university faculties in the United States and that the total number of nurse-midwives in this country at the present time is 209.[3]

[3] Helen Fisk, Chairman of Nurse and Midwife Section of the *National Organization of Public Health Nurses,* May 20, 1946.

CHAPTER VI

ORGANIZATION AND LICENSURE OF NURSE-MIDWIVES

American Association of Nurse-Midwives

Nurse-midwives had been working in the United States only a little over three years when the first organization was formed in Kentucky in 1928. It was initiated by a group of the nurses working with the Frontier Nursing Service, the only place where a group of nurse-midwives was employed at that time, and was called the *Kentucky State Association of Midwives, Incorporated.* The first meeting was held at Hyden Hospital on October 7, 1928 and the purpose was stated as follows:

> The nature of the business proposed to be transacted, promoted and carried on by this corporation shall be to foster, encourage, and, in the qualifications for its own membership, to maintain a high standard of midwifery with special reference to rugged, difficult and economically poor areas; to do this in cooperation with the State Board of Health and the officers thereof, and in cooperation with the medical and nursing professions and with other like-minded citizens and organizations; and thereby to raise the standard of midwives and nurse-midwives, who are or have been or may hereafter be engaged in the active practice of midwifery, to a standard not lower than the official standards required by first class European countries in 1929.[1]

Regulations for membership were prescribed and power was vested in a Board of Directors consisting of seven persons to be elected each year at the annual meeting, to act when the Association was not in session.[2]

In 1933, at its annual meeting the Association chose for its seal the Kentucky cardinal and his mate in a natural setting surrounded by the Title of the Association and the year of its incorporation. With the permission of the Midwives Institute in London, the

[1] "Kentucky State Association of Midwives, Inc.," *The Quarterly Bulletin of the Frontier Nursing Service, Inc.,* XVI, No. 4 (1939), p. 19.

[2] *Ibid.,* p. 20.

motto: "Life is the gift of God," was chosen. This is the English translation of their Latin motto.[3]

Annual meetings were held, usually on Thanksgiving Day, at Wendover, the Headquarters of the Frontier Nursing Service and since all of its members but one were Frontier Nursing Service staff members, it was a convenient time and place. In 1938 there were forty-four members.[4]

In October 1941 because of war and necessary changes, the need for altered membership requirements, name and purpose, prompted the members to change their title to the American Association of Nurse-Midwives and to revise its articles of Incorporation. Dorothy F. Buck, R.N., S.C.M., Secretary of the Association, wrote in 1942 as follows: "With the increased interest in the nurse-midwife in the United States, the Association has striven to show by its new name and certain changes in its Articles of Incorporation that its interest also is not sectional. Its object remains unchanged . . . ."[5]

All nurse-midwives in this country were invited to become members and by 1942 seventy-six nurses had responded. Annual meetings are still held at Wendover, Kentucky, but since the membership has expanded to include nurse-midwives from all areas, there was some discussion at the 1946 meeting about having the meetings in different places from year to year in order to make it possible for all members to attend.[6]

The central office of the American Association of Nurse-Midwives is located at Hyden, Kentucky. Mrs. Breckinridge has always been president of the Association.[7]

Nurse-Midwife Section of the National Organization for Public Health Nursing

For several years nurse-midwives have believed that they should be represented in a national nursing organization. There was no

[3] *Ibid.*

[4] *Ibid.*

[5] "American Association of Nurse-Midwives," *The Quarterly Bulletin of the Frontier Nursing Service, Inc.,* XVII, No. 4 (1942).

[6] Minutes of the Annual Meeting, September 28, 1945.

[7] Information obtained from Dorothy Buck.

national professional organization to specify standards of qualifications, education, or practice and the need for this resulted in the formation of the Nurse-Midwifery Section of the National Organization for Public Health Nursing at the Annual meeting of that organization on October 2, 1944. Helen Fisk, R.N., C.N.M., Chief of the Division of Public Health Nursing in Maryland, was elected Chairman of the Section and Hattie Hemschemeyer, R.N., C.N.M., Director of the organization, became the Vice-Chairman.

The chief purpose of the new Section is to interpret the aims of nurse-midwifery to members of the medical and nursing professions, to study and set standards for nurse-midwifery training and practice, and to investigate the need for nurse-midwives and the ways in which nurses with this special training can be used to promote maternal and infant health.[8]

Ruth Doran, R.N., C.N.M., General Nursing Consultant of the Children's Bureau, was appointed chairman of a nominating committee for executive members. The executive committee was appointed in the fall of 1945. The members are:

Helen Fisk, R.N., C.N.M., Chairman; Hattie Hemschemeyer, R.N., C.N.M., Vice-Chairman; Hazel Corbin, R.N., Lucille Petry, R.N., Ruth Taylor, R.N., Sister M. Theophane Shoemaker, R.N., C.N.M., Frances Fell, R.N., S.C.M., Catherine Lory, R.N., C.M., Sara E. Fetter, R.N., C.N.M., George W. Kosmak, M.D., Robert H. Riley, M.D., Nicholoson Eastman, M.D., and Miss Agnes Fuller, Secretary.

Three subcommittees were appointed and objectives were determined for their activities:

1. To study and set standards of practice for nurse-midwives.
2. To study and promote new opportunities in the field of nurse-midwifery.
3. To study and evaluate standards for schools of nurse-midwifery.[9]

[8] "Nurse-Midwives Organize," *Briefs,* IX, No. 2 (1944). "Nurse-Midwife Section of the National Organization for Public Health Nursing." *Public Health Nursing* XXXVI (1944), p. 254.

[9] Report of Dorothy Buck at the Eighteenth Annual Meeting of the American Association of Nurse-Midwives.

The subcommittees have already met and at the next meeting of the National Organization for Public Health Nursing which will be held in September 1946, their reports will be read.

Licensure of Nurse-Midwives

New Mexico is the only state that has enacted laws providing specifically for the licensure of nurse-midwives. On August 4, 1945, the law became effective in New Mexico and it designates that the applicant must be a graduate nurse registered or eligible for registration in New Mexico who has completed a course in a school of midwifery meeting the standards set by the Nurse-Midwife Section of the National Organization for Public Health Nursing. Permits to practice are issued through the Director of the New Mexico State Department of Health.

The law provides that the "nurse-midwife may care for normal patients who have received adequate prenatal examination by a licensed physician whose knowledge of obstetrics is deemed adequate by the Department of Public Health. She must comply with all standing orders issued by the Health Department."[10] The law also specifies the conditions under which the license may be revoked.

Several other States, although they have no law, have made special arrangements for examinations to be administered to nurse-midwives wishing to practice in the States, and they are licensed under the law provided for the indigenous midwives. This gives them legal status and affords a protection to the nurse.[11]

---

[10] *Nurse-Midwife Regulations for New Mexico.* (State of New Mexico Department of Public Health, 1945.)

[11] Analysis of letters received from Director of Nursing in State Health Departments.

CONCLUSION

This study has served to emphasize the fact that in the United State nurse-midwifery is still in a pioneer stage of development. Diversified efforts have been made by private and public agencies to demonstrate the usefulness of the well prepared nurse-midwife in a program of complete maternity care; some of these demonstrations have been successful but a great many of them have not.

It is evident that wherever a direct delivery service has been organized for nurse-midwife practice or wherever nurse-midwives have been engaged in a program of supervision for native midwives, their services were accepted willingly by the people. Demand for the service was proof that it filled a real need. The reasons for success or lack of success, therefore, do not lie in the province of felt need; they must be sought for in the fundamental processes of selection of students and their preparation, in the organization of nurse-midwife programs, and in professional relationships.

The author recommends that studies be made to determine: 1. Those personal and professional qualifications which are required for successful experience as a nurse-midwife; 2. What the curriculum for nurse-midwifery preparation should be in light of the duties such professional services impose; 3. What types of organization are conducive to permanency for nurse-midwife practice; 4. How desirable professional relationships which will promote the welfare of the patient and at the same time stimulate prudent initiative and contentment in the nurse-midwives can be developed.

BIBLIOGRAPHY

BOOKS

Hooker, Ransom S., M.D. *Maternal Mortality in New York City*. New York: The Commonwealth Fund, 1933.

Maternity Center Association 1918-1943. Maternity Center Association, New York: 1943.

Obstetric Education. Report of the subcommittee on obstetric teaching and education. New York: The Century Co., 1932.

Public Health Nursing in Obstetrics, Part 1. New York: Maternity Center Association, 1941 (revised).

ARTICLES

"Advanced Maternity Nursing," *Public Health Nursing*, XXXII (1932), p. 16.

"At Home," *Public Health Nursing*, XIX (1927), pp. 606-607.

Baker, S. Josephine, M.D. "The Functions of the Midwife," *The Woman's Medical Journal*, XXIII (1913), pp. 196-197.

Beard, Mary. "Midwifery in England," *Public Health Nursing*, XVIII (1926), pp. 634-640.

Briefs. (Publication of the Maternity Center Association, New York.) (1936-1945). Vols. I, II, III, IV, V, VI, VII, VIII, IX, X.

Buck, Dorothy F. "The Nurses on Horseback Ride On," *The American Journal of Nursing*, XL (1940), pp. 993-995.

Caffin, Freda and Caroline. "Experiences of the Nurse-Midwife in the Kentucky Mountains," *The Nation's Health*, VIII (1926), pp. 801-803.

"Concerning the Nurse-Midwife," *Public Health Nursing*, XVIII (1926), p. 526.

Corbin, Hazel. "Maternity Nursing," *The Trained Nurse and Hospital Review*, (1929).

————. "Nurse-Midwives for Tomorrow," *Trained Nurse and Hospital Review*, CIX (1942), pp. 167-169.

————. "Teaching the Public About Maternity," *Public Health Nursing*, XXXI (1939), pp. 596-602.

"Course for Nurse-Midwives," *The American Journal of Nursing*, XL (1940), p. 335.

Davis, Carl Henry, M.D. "Obstetrics and Gynecology in General Practice," *The American Journal of Nursing*, XXIX (1943), p. 1443.

61

DeLee, Joseph B., M.D. "Meddlesome Midwifery in Renaissance," *The Journal of the American Medical Association,* LXVII (1916), pp. 1126-1129.

————. "Obstetrics Versus Midwifery," *The Journal of the American Medical Association,* CIII (1934), p. 307.

Deutsch, Naomi. "Economic Aspects of Maternal Care," *Public Health Nursing,* XXXI (1939), pp. 619-624.

Edgar, J. Clifton, M.D. "Why the Midwife?" *The American Journal of Obstetrics and Gynecology,* LXXVIII (1918), pp. 242-255.

Editorial. "Lack of Care of American Mothers," *The American Journal of Nursing,* XXVI (1926), pp. 297-298.

Emmons, Arthur Brewster, M.D. and Huntington, James Lincoln, M.D. "The Midwife," *The American Journal of Obstetrics and Diseases of Women and Children,* LXV (1912).

Fell, Frances. "A Midwifery Delivery Service," *The American Journal of Nursing,* XLIII (1943).

Ferguson, Elizabeth. "Midwifery Supervision," *Public Health Nursing,* XXX (1938), pp. 482-485.

French, William J., M.D. "Place of Maternal and Child Health in a Generalized Program in a Health Unit." *The American Journal of Public Health,* XXXI (1941), pp. 465-470.

Hall, Carrie M. "Training the Obstetrical Nurse," *The American Journal of Nursing,* XXVII (1927), pp. 373-379.

Hemschemeyer, Hattie. "A Training School for Nurse Midwives," *The American Journal of Nursing,* XXXII (1932), p. 374.

Jeidell, Helmina, M.D. and Fricke, Willa M., M.D. "The Midwives of Anne Arundel County, Maryland," *Johns Hopkins Hospital Report,* XXIII (1912), pp. 279-281.

Hemschemeyer, Hattie, R.N. "Midwifery in the United States," *The American Journal of Nursing,* XXXIX (1939), pp. 1181-1187.

Joint Committee of the National League of Nursing Education and National Organization of Public Health Nursing. "Advanced Obstetric Nursing," *The American Journal of Nursing,* XLI (1941), pp. 945-948.

Kelly, Florence. "The Maternity Bill," *Public Health Nursing,* XIII (1921), p. 284.

Kentucky Committee for Mothers and Babies. (Publication of the Kentucky Committee for Mothers and Babies, Inc.) Vol. I (1925).

Kosmak, George W., M.D. "Community Responsibilities for Safeguarding Motherhood," *Public Health Nursing,* XXVI (1934), pp. 292-299.

————. "The Trained Nurse and the Midwife," *The American Journal of Nursing,* XXXIV (1934), pp. 421-423.

Knox, J. H. Mason, M.D. "The Situation of Midwives in the Counties of Maryland," *Public Health Nursing*, XVIII (1926), pp. 409-410.

Lenroot, Katherine F. *The Children's Bureau*, U. S. Department of Labor, 1937.

Lester, Betty, R.N. "The Experiences of a Midwifery Supervisor in the Kentucky Hills," *The American Journal of Nursing*, XXXI (1931), pp. 573-577.

Logan, Alice. "The Nurse-Midwife in Leslie County, Kentucky," *Public Health Nursing*, XVIII (1926), pp. 542-546.

"Mary Breckinridge, R.N. Nurse-Midwife," *The American Journal of Nursing*, XXX (1930), pp. 311-312.

Marriner, Jessie. "Midwifery in Alabama," *Public Health Nurse*, XVIII (1926), pp. 128-131.

"Maternal Mortality in England," *Public Health Nursing*, XXVI (1924), p. 672.

McCord, James R., M.D. "The Education of Midwives," *The American Journal of Obstetrics and Gynecology*, XXI (1931), pp. 837-852.

"Midwifery in Kentucky," *The American Journal of Nursing*, XXV (1925), p. 1004.

"News Notes," *Public Health Nursing*, XX (1928), p. 612.

"News Notes," *Public Health Nursing*, XVII (1925), p. 224.

National League of Nursing Education. "A Report of a Study Made on the Need for Nurses to Study Midwifery and its Recommendations," *Thirty-third Report of the National League of Nursing Education*, (1927), pp. 231-236.

Noyes, Clara D., R.N. "Training of Midwives in Relation to the Prevention of Infant Mortality," *The American Journal of Obstetrics and Diseases of Women and Children*, LXVI (1912), pp. 1051-1059.

Pagaud, Mary V. "The Next Steps in Maternity Nursing," *Public Health Nursing*, XX (1928), pp. 622-625.

Quarterly Bulletin of the Frontier Nursing Service, Inc., Vols. IV-XXI inclusive (1928-1945).

Quarterly Bulletin of the Kentucky Committee for Mothers and Babies, Inc., Vols. II-III (1926-1927).

Rand, Winifred. "Impressions of a Public Health Nursing Service in the Kentucky Mountains," *The American Journal of Nursing*, XXIX (1929), pp. 527-530.

Rockstroh, Edna C. "Enter—the Nurse-Midwife," *The American Journal of Nursing*, XXVII (1927), pp. 159-164.

Rude, Anna E., M.D. "The Midwife Problem in the United States," a printed copy of a paper read before the Section on Obstetrics and Gynecology and Abdominal Surgery, June 1923, in San Francisco.

Taussig, Fred J., M.D. *The Nurse Midwife.* A paper presented at the Second Annual Meeting of the National Organization of Public Health Nurses. April 25, 1914, in printed form.

"The Committee on the Costs of Medical Care Reports," *The American Journal of Nursing,* XXXII (1932), pp. 1286-1291.

Watson, Benjamin P., M.D. "Can Our Methods of Obstetric Practice be Improved?" *The American Journal of Nursing,* XXXI (1931), pp. 499-500.

Wile, Ira S., M.D. "Schools for Midwives," *Medical Record,* LXXXI (1912).

Willeford, Mary B., "The Frontier Nursing Service," *Public Health Nursing,* XXV (1933), pp. 6-10.

Williams, J. Whitridge, M.D. "Medical Education and the Midwife Problem in the United States," *The Journal of the American Medical Association,* LVIII (1912), pp. 1-7.

Ziegler, Charles Edward, M.D. "The Elimination of the Midwife," *The Journal of the American Medical Association,* LX (1913).

BULLETINS

Announcement of the *School of Nurse-Midwifery Maternity Center Association,* New York: Maternity Center Association.

Bulletin of the *Tuskegee School of Nurse-Midwifery,* Alabama: Tuskegee Institute, 1945.

Frontier Graduate School of Midwifery, Hyden, Kentucky, 1944.

School for Nurse-Midwifery, Santa Fe Catholic Maternity Institute. (Mimeographed announcement.)

Special Delivery M. C. A. Alumnae Everywhere, Vol. I, Nos. 1-2.

Minutes of the Seventeenth Annual Meeting of the American Association of Nurse-Midwives, Incorporated. September 28, 1944.

Minutes of the Eighteenth Annual Meeting of the American Association of Nurse-Midwives, Incorporated. September 28, 1945.

UNPUBLISHED MATERIAL

American Association of Nurse-Midwives, Incorporated, Amended Articles of Incorporation, October 1941. (Mimeographed.)

By-Laws of the Nurse-Midwifery Section of the National Organization for Public Health Nursing, Inc.

Nurse-Midwife Regulations for New Mexico. New Mexico Board of Public Health, 1945.

CPSIA information can be obtained
at www.ICGtesting.com
Printed in the USA
LVOW10s1955290118
564491LV00017B/63/P